REVOLUTIONIZING QUALITY OF LIFE IN LONG-TERM CARE

The
PERSON-CENTERED
Way

James H. Collins, Ph.D.

Copyright © 2009 James H. Collins, Ph.D.
All rights reserved.

ISBN: 1-4392-4614-9
ISBN-13: 9781439246146
Library of Congress Control Number: 2009906030

CONTENTS

ACKNOWLEDGEMENTS. v

INTRODUCTION ix

CHAPTER ONE:. 1
Getting Started

CHAPTER TWO: 15
Culture Change and Creating a Home

CHAPTER THREE: 27
The Importance of Food and the Dining Experience

CHAPTER FOUR: 49
Activities and Quality of Life

CHAPTER FIVE: 63
Changes in the Delivery of Care

CHAPTER SIX: 77
From an Institution to a Home: Environmental Changes

CHAPTER SEVEN: 91
Creating a New Culture of Dementia Care

CHAPTER EIGHT: **105**
Introducing "Family-Centered Care"

CHAPTER NINE: **115**
Can We Afford Person-Centered Care?

CHAPTER TEN: **131**
How Regulations Support Person-Centered Care
and Culture Change

CHAPTER ELEVEN: **147**
The Necessity of Leadership in Culture Change

CHAPTER TWELVE: **163**
The Benefits of Person-Centered Care and Culture Change

CHAPTER THIRTEEN: **173**
Concluding Remarks

ACKNOWLEDGEMENTS

I am grateful to so many wonderful people who have helped me along the way in writing this book. First, I wish to thank all of the residents who I have observed and interviewed. Without their help, this book would have no purpose. I also want to thank the many family members of residents whom I interviewed and had many spontaneous conversations with in numerous long-term care facilities. I am indebted to the hundreds of employees, managers, supervisors, and administrative staff who allowed me into their world as a researcher. They provided me with so much of the information in this book.

I also want to thank my family. To my wife Anabel, thank you for the constant inspiration and encouragement when I didn't feel like I had anything to offer and wasn't ready to put words on paper. You always said, "You will do it when you are inspired, and I know you will be." To my mother Mary, a nursing assistant for thirty years, who started in 1972 making $1.50 an hour: You took care of residents for three decades, loved your job, and never complained. I truly look up to you. I also want to thank my little girl, Karina Bella, who ripped the V and B buttons and the space bar off of my laptop and

Daddy still got this book done! I am a much better typist thanks to you! I also want to thank my older daughters Elena and Celia and my sisters Constance and Patricia for all of their love and support through this and so many other projects.

I want to thank Dionne Nichol for her insight, patience with me, and compassion for her staff and residents. She is truly one of the best administrators I have ever met. Thank you for allowing me to observe your staff and residents, interview them, hold focus groups, and have access to your facility. Her director of nursing, Joyce Hoover, was very helpful and brought a fresh perspective to my work. Melanie Ripley, thank you for your kind and compassionate approach to your staff and residents and for giving me access to your staff and facility. I want to give a very special thanks to Terry Willingham, the most talented, creative, and potentially insane activity director I have ever met! You gave me a completely different perspective on activities and giving residents both meaning and purpose in their lives. Your work is incredible.

I am very grateful to the staff at Country View of Sunbury located in Sunbury, Ohio, for all of their help, especially Matt Dapore, LNHA, and Sherry Gallion, RN, Director of Nursing. They truly know what person-centered care is all about and live it each and every day in their beautiful long-term care home. Another long-term care administrator, Bryan Casey, is a great man to whom I owe many thanks as well. He is a gentleman and a professional who is guided by a deep and genuine love for his residents and ensures high standards as well as a great quality of living in his homes.

Many thanks to Mark Grippi, LNHA, and Chef Will Rosch, who have been fearless pioneers in person-centered care and culture change. I admire their courage to step away from the norm and do what their gut tells them to do in their home. They have greatly improved the lives of so many residents and employees, and I have been lucky enough to watch them in action.

I also want to thank all of the healthcare professionals who have attended my seminars, workshops, training sessions, and in-services over the past sixteen years. I have enjoyed all of the stories and wisdom passed on to me throughout the years from all of you. You have taught me many things, but one of the most important lessons I have learned is that you never know how much you don't know until you talk to other people who do know.

I offer my deepest thanks to an incredible man who has vision and talent like none other in the nursing home industry—Brian Colleran. You have given countless residents a wonderful place to call home and have provided employees with a culture for which to be thankful and of which to be proud. You encourage people to think and act on their own and to be the best that they can be. In a very powerful way, you have created a culture of compassion that is widespread, genuine, and lasting. I owe you countless thanks.

INTRODUCTION

Person-centered care is the most innovative and exciting way to dramatically improve both quality of care and quality of life because it makes the resident first, above and beyond everything else that takes place in long-term care. It provides a road map and acts as a driving philosophy for deinstitutionalizing the place where so many elderly and medically compromised people find themselves—in a nursing home. Person-centered care offers a number of exciting changes to each department in the facility—from nursing to dietary services, social services, activities, and housekeeping. There is almost no limit to the modifications that can be made with this new paradigm. Facilities all over the country are implementing person-centered care features or are just learning about it now. Some facilities may be reluctant to try a person-centered care program of their own. To those I say, if you don't learn, believe in, and implement person-centered care in your facility soon, you will be twenty years behind every long-term care facility in the country that does provide person-centered care. Elderly and medically compromised people deserve better. There is a better way to create a place that feels like home with care that feels like love and provide a life that is worth living. This is the "Person-Centered Way."

This book provides the tools you need to understand person-centered care and start your own brand of it within your facility. I have written this book after years of research and observation in long-term care facilities. Hundreds of residents, family members, and employees have provided me with their ideas, opinions, and concerns about person-centered care. I have trained hundreds of employees in dozens of nursing homes on the philosophies, values, and the nuts-and-bolts of getting this model of care started in their buildings. After experiencing years of research and hands-on training, I feel that it's time to put all of these ideas in this book. I hope that you will read this book with as much enthusiasm and passion as I have written it, and then take this information to the next level by using it in your facility to greatly improve the quality of not only care but life itself for those individuals who live in your facility.

Believe me, understanding and implementing person-centered care will be no walk in the park. Even though you may read this book and believe in the ideas presented within it, getting your staff to erase years of doing things the old-fashioned way and abandon the medical model of providing care will be challenging. Some employees may wish to hold onto the idea that the building is their place of employment and not the home of the residents who live there. Everyone who is presented with the ideas in this book will ultimately have to see the need to change how things are done in the nursing home and engage in changing the culture of the facility. When presenting person-centered care to your staff, residents, or families, it should be done in a motivational, energetic, and moving way. It is a refreshing change away from an overly institutionalized way of life to one that is much closer to living at home, being surrounded by people who love to provide care and will try each day to provide purpose in the lives of those they serve.

WHAT IS PERSON-CENTERED CARE?

An Attitude

A great place to start learning about person-centered care and how it improves long-term care is getting a grasp on some basic definitions. Person-centered care is an attitude maintaining that the resident is more important than providing nursing tasks, following rigid care schedules and routines, and doing other forms of work. The person is first, and everything else is second—period. I believe person-centered care is more than just a model of care—it involves adopting an attitude that puts the resident first. Scheduled medication passes, treatments, and the times meals and activities are provided are all secondary to what matters most—the needs and quality of life of the resident. Long-term care has been dominated by schedules, regiments, routines, and task-driven ideologies since nursing homes have existed. It can be argued that these methods of care were adopted from hospitals, but elderly and frail individuals living in a facility they call their "home" should not be dominated by hospital-like living.

A Philosophy

Person-centered care is also a philosophy that involves a departure from institutional life and providing care according to the traditional medical model. It is a move towards more natural, social, and personalized ways of living—not in an institution, but in a home or house. Institutional life can be characterized as a set pattern of group living where the individual becomes lost within the larger group. This is particularly evident during morning wake-up and a.m. care rounds, medication passes, meal times, activities, shower and bath schedules, and p.m. care rounds. Such tasks are developed to maintain order in caring for a large group of people. Systems and routines are created to assist the masses as well as make work convenient for employees.

Although there is a long tradition of this kind of care in nursing homes, as well as hospitals, group homes and some assisted living facilities, the focus is on the work at hand and not the resident. It is very institutional to wake residents up too early, get them ready, take them to the dining room, seat them, and watch them fall asleep at the table because breakfast will not be served for another thirty minutes. This way of life is far removed from the ebb and flow of natural living, which involves allowing residents to wake up naturally, pass medications when they are ready for them, provide meals when they want to eat as well as food that they want to eat, and allow them to enjoy each day as they want.

A Road Map

Person-centered care can also be seen as a road map that provides direction for management, employees, residents, and families to get started in the process and continue forging ahead with new and exciting ideas, changes, and plans for creating a person-centered home. In this sense, person-centered care identifies various aspects of long-term care that can be modified or changed. Employees will develop a new vision statement for their own brand of person-centered care in their facility. This vision statement acts as a driving force behind their efforts. The road map paradigm also provides guidance concerning which areas of care require change, including nursing care, meals, and activities. It can also be very helpful in deciding which modifications to make in the physical design and structure of the building, such as removing nurses' stations and creating enhanced resident living space.

OTHER DEFINITIONS AND THOUGHTS ON PERSON-CENTERED CARE

A Process

I would be remiss not to include a sample of some of the literature that has been written on person-centered care and its meaning. Dawn Brooker wrote an excellent book called *Person-Centered Dementia Care: Making*

Services Better, which outlines what she calls the VIPS Approach (pp. 11-13). She describes four essential elements of person centered care: Valuing, Individuals, Perspective, and Social. *Valuing* involves the caregiver adopting the attitude that individuals diagnosed with dementia have the same rights as anyone else and should live a good life. Residents should also be treated not in batches, but as *individuals* who each have their own life history, unique personality, and social experience. Caregivers should attempt to understand the resident's world view and see life through their eyes and from their *perspective*. And lastly, *social* aspects of life are important but are unfortunately lacking in long-term care. Elements of social life include close and meaningful relationships and friendships, bringing the community into the facility, throwing parties and celebrations, and normalizing life in other social ways that enhance the well-being of residents, families, and employees.

Person-centered care is viewed in the literature as a process where the end result and ultimate goal is the well-being of the resident (Tallis-Nayak, p. 46). Care is not viewed as a means to an end but instead is an ongoing process where the focus is not on the task but the well-being of the individual receiving care. This view of person-centered care can be interpreted to mean that comfort, happiness, and quality of life are much more important than the technical or mechanical aspects of providing care. Traditional long-term care involves routines and tasks that are inarguably indispensable, but they should never supersede the psychosocial needs of the resident.

Another way to look at person-centered care is offered by Rantz and Flesner, who focus on personal control, choice, and freedom it provides. They believe, "The basic goal of person-centered care is to create a place where people go to live and enjoy the rest of their lives. Person-centered care focuses on providing individualized care to meet the needs of the residents [who are] encouraged to be in control of their lives, with the freedom to make choices about their routines and schedules, remaining as independent as they want to be and as their health allows" (p. 15-16). This definition stresses the importance of residents living their lives as they choose, making decisions concerning their care, and developing a sense of security and comfort in their home. Tasks and work are not emphasized in this definition. Rather, living a satisfying life is most desirable and can lead to a higher level of physical, psychological, social, and spiritual well-being.

Summary of Person-Centered Definitions

It is hoped that the reader has gained a basic idea of what person-centered care is as an attitude, philosophy, road map, and process. As an attitude, person-centered care involves developing a *feeling* about the quality of care and life that residents deserve. The attitude is that the resident comes first and everything else comes second. In terms of a philosophy, person-centered care is a way of *thinking* about the resident as an important and valuable human being who should feel like they are living in their own home, not an institution or the employee's workplace. The road map concept is valuable as a guide in getting started and making your way successfully through different changes you decide to make in the facility. And last, person-centered care is an ongoing process—one that never ends, but always changes and evolves. There is no true end point to person-centered care. It will always change as residents come and go.

Breaking Away from the Past

It is important to understand what person-centered care is, but it is equally important to understand why it is necessary in improving the quality of care and life in long-term care. For many years, nursing home life has been characterized as institutionalized, routine-driven, task-oriented, overly medicalized, and non-home-like. The resident does not come first in traditional long-term care, but is instead secondary to employee schedules, technical aspects of care, dietary and activity calendars, and decisions made by management. It is therefore important to appreciate where long-term care has come from, where it is, and where person-centered care can take it in the very near future.

Nursing Homes as Total Institutions

Nursing homes can be categorized as "total institutions," a term first used by the sociologist and theorist Erving Goffman in his groundbreaking book *Asylums: Essays on the Social Situation of Mental Patients and other Inmates.* He writes, "A total institution may be defined as a place of residence and work where a large number of like-situated individuals, cut off from the wider society for an appreciable period of time, together lead an enclosed, formally administered round of life" (p. xii).

Although Goffman refers to life in a mental institution during the late 1950s and early 1960s, the concept can be applied to nursing homes, prisons, boarding schools, and monasteries today. According to this definition, nursing homes are total institutions for obvious reasons: a large number of residents live in them, an equally large group of employees work in them, many residents have similar diagnoses and medical conditions (i.e., Alzheimer's, depression, cardiovascular disease, diabetes, etc.), residents may live in nursing homes for a very long time, they may not be involved in life outside of the facility, society is largely cut off from the facility, and they live according to rules, regulations, policies, and schedules developed and implemented by a paid, administrative staff.

Although Goffman's concept is over forty years old, it applies today to the traditional nursing home. So, where do we go from here? One way to look at this situation is that total institutions are the problem and person-centered care is the answer to the problem. Therefore, it is important to understand that we must break away from the past and educate employees and families from that from which we are breaking away.

SOME NEGATIVE ASPECTS OF NURSING HOME LIFE

Group Care vs. Individual Care

Traditional nursing home care has developed a number of characteristics and aspects that can have a negative impact on the lives of residents. While some of these have evolved unintentionally, others are traits or features of total institutions and can be greatly improved with person-centered care. Goffman wasn't alone in his observation that people living in total institutions are treated as one large group and not as unique individuals with preferences concerning their care and life in general. Kahana described living in nursing homes as "batch treatment," where house rules apply to all residents and individual differences are not very important (p. 51). Although Kahana wrote this in 1971, it holds true today and is evidenced by the use of wake-up lists, early morning medication passes and treatments, scheduled meal times for breakfast, lunch, dinner, and snacks, shower schedules, scheduled activities, and visits by ancillary specialists—just to name a few.

This type of care is not person-centered because it does not allow differentiation between individuals. Instead, it treats all residents as one large homogeneous group. Although it may be easier or more convenient to deliver care in this manner, not all residents wish to live their lives according to a schedule created and imposed by someone else. This type of care creates routines and a mundane flow of life in the facility. It is difficult to live naturally and at one's own pace when there is a schedule superimposed on one's life. Residents and employees may become institutionalized due to this kind of care and disciplined and regimented schedules. Group care is also lacking because there is no flexibility for natural living, no freedom of choice, and decisions have been removed from the individual and have already been made by management.

Loss

A universal problem in long-term living is, without question, that of loss. Elderly and medically compromised individuals experience many losses prior to being admitted to a nursing home, and unfortunately the number of losses continues to add up. The resident may lose his or her home, car, savings, connection to the outside world, family and friends, a comfortable and familiar lifestyle, as well as independence and physical mobility. Possible losses that can occur in the nursing home include those of privacy, dignity, autonomy, social life, self-worth, and the feeling of "home." Many authors have addressed the theme of loss in long-term care. Savishinsky documents how residents lost contact with the community and became forgotten people (p. 238). Lidtz, et al. (pp. 170-172), and Kane, et al., (p. 164) stress how residents lose their standard of living, privacy, and independence.

Person-centered care can assist in compensating for these losses and many more. Privacy is viewed as the right of all residents, and the facility should accommodate for private and customized living spaces as well as private areas where residents can be alone or enjoy the company of their family and friends without disruption. Autonomy and independence are hallmarks of person-centered care, and resident choice is viewed as a necessity. Residents have the right to choose how their care is delivered, when it is delivered, when they wish to wake up and go to bed, when they prefer taking a bath or shower, what they want to eat, how much, when and where they eat, and so on. Understandably, person-centered care is not a cure-all for loss, but it can significantly help to compensate for many of the losses that residents experience.

Other Negative Aspects

Besides being treated in groups and experiencing numerous losses, residents may be subjected to a variety of undignified experiences in the facility. Nursing assistants may become used to working on bodies and beds instead of human beings with unique personalities, needs, and preferences. This may occur particularly when staff is running short due to call offs. Case loads may be high and staffing may be low, and as a consequence, care must be quick and impersonal.

Residents may feel dehumanized, depersonalized, or that they may be losing individuality, identity, or sense of self. They may not be able to celebrate their cultural or ethnic background. Some residents may become depressed because they must share a room with a roommate who is very ill, dying, demented, or abusive. They may be labeled by the staff as problematic, difficult, non-compliant, or worse, "crazy" or "psychotic." Residents can experience episodes that are degrading and humiliating. Others may wish to withdraw from the life of the facility because it is all too much for them. Staff may treat adult residents like children or babies, infantilize them, or intimidate them into compliance. Residents on certain units (i.e., Alzheimer's unit, geropsychiatric unit) may be stigmatized and feel banished to their living space. Residents who are slow or diagnosed with neurological disorders may feel that direct-care employees outpace them during hands-on care.

The bottom line is there are numerous aspects and characteristics of long-term care that are negative, undignified, and humiliating, all of which can have damaging consequences on the lives of elderly and frail individuals. Person-centered care can help change this negative culture by respecting and appreciating each resident as a unique person and getting to know the person not as a resident in need of care, but as a complete human being with needs, preferences, and a rich life history. Implementing person-centered care can replace dehumanization with humanization, and depersonalization with personalization. It can provide a new perspective to see residents not as diagnoses or disorders, but as people who have special needs and challenges. They are not labels—they are people.

Person-centered care can put decision-making, power, and control back into the hands of the individuals who should have it—the residents. They should be treated like adults because they are adults, not children or infants, regardless of physical or cognitive disability. They have the right to refuse care and make choices regarding their care and life. Each day can bring new reasons to wake up with purpose and meaning. Their lives, emotions, and needs can be validated with person-centered care.

Adding It Up

Thus far we have explored various definitions of person-centered care, identifying it as an attitude, philosophy, road map for change, and a process of providing care. It is essential to understand what person-centered care is so that these perspectives can be adopted and put to real use in the facility. It is also important to understand that regardless of intentions or blame, there are many negative aspects of long-term care that require change. Person-centered care is the vehicle of change that so many healthcare professionals have been seeking throughout their careers. Elderly and frail individuals deal with loss before they enter the facility and then face more losses with each passing day. Many negative aspects of traditional long-term care can have seriously damaging effects on the individual's self-esteem and quality of life. This is why person-centered care is so important. It can help management and employees develop a new vision of care, provide families with confidence that their loved ones will feel at home, and give residents purpose and meaning in life. These goals sound pretty big—and they are. They are also very attainable. Chapter One explains how to start the process and develop your own customized brand of person-centered care in your facility.

POINTS TO PONDER

1. After reading this chapter, how do you feel about your facility? Is it more of a total institution than a person-centered home?

2. Do you and your staff believe that person-centered care can significantly improve both the quality of care as well as quality of life in your facility?

3. Are your residents treated more like a group of people or as distinct and unique individuals?

CHAPTER ONE: GETTING STARTED

Tell me and I'll forget, show me and I may remember, involve me and I will understand.

Chinese Proverb

One of the most challenging aspects of person-centered care is getting started. It can be compared to starting your own exercise program—it's difficult to get started and develop a new pattern of behavior, but once you get things in motion, you are on the road to success. Before I address starting the process, I want to discuss what we are planning to start. There are a number of areas in the facility that will require examination and change. Some of these will seem obvious and making certain modifications will not be that difficult, while others may be more covert and change may not seem necessary, desirable, or achievable. What you and your staff will engage in is culture change. But before jumping into changing the culture, it is important to examine the elements of the culture that require change.

Eight Critical Components of Person-Centered Care

Based on a review of the literature and my own observations in long-term care facilities, I have developed eight components of person-centered care that can help with the organization and implementation of person-centered care in your facility. These components are meant to provide areas for you and your staff to think about before getting the process started. They offer a road map in person-centered culture change.

The eight components are:
1. A change in employee attitudes about long-term care and the development of a new philosophy towards quality of care and quality of life.
2. Changes in food choice and how dining is experienced.
3. The inclusion of activities that provide purpose and meaning, personal growth, and contribution to community.
4. Changes in the delivery of direct care by the nursing staff.
5. Environmental changes and modification of living spaces in the facility.
6. Changes in how dementia care is viewed and delivered.
7. Partnerships between long-term care homes, families and the broader community.

8. Changes in leadership and management styles that promote autonomy, creativity, and self-directed employees.

After looking at these critical elements of person-centered care, you may be saying, "This is a lot to do and is going to take a long time to get done!" To this I reply: "You're right!" There is a lot of work ahead of you and your staff, but it is necessary so that, in the end, you will create a place where employees love to work and residents love to live. This is work that is honorable and will improve quality of care and living for individuals who deserve it.

Somebody once said "anything worth doing takes time," and this is absolutely true concerning person-centered care. Managers, employees, residents, and families may become frustrated and doubt that the benefits will outweigh the costs involved in so much change. Some will be naysayers from the very start. I would be lying if I told you this will be easy. I have outlined the Eight Components as a way to break down person-centered care and culture change into more manageable parts of the process. Sit down with your residents and staff and determine which one you will begin. Which area requires the most change immediately? If you are ever in doubt—ask your residents! They will tell you what areas of care and the facility need immediate attention.

Introduce the Idea to Staff and Families

Once you feel comfortable with your understanding of person-centered care and culture change, it is time to introduce these ideas to your staff and families. I recommend holding a large in-service meeting to make staff aware that the facility is learning about person-centered care and that they will soon be engaging in making significant and lasting changes in how care is delivered, how food and the dining experience will be improved, how activities will be enhanced, and how the facility will soon become a home. I would deliver this information with great enthusiasm, excitement, and passion. Get your staff energized about person-centered care. In so many of my training sessions, I have been told by hundreds of employees, "Finally! This is how I have always wanted to provide care to my residents." Many healthcare professionals have exclaimed, "This is why I went into health care in the first place!" It is now time for you to validate why you and your staff are in long-term care and why we have all chosen this path in our professional lives.

The next step, in my opinion, is to set up a training schedule utilizing the "learning circle" method. Learning circles are very effective for training employees in new concepts and especially in person-centered care. They involve limiting a training session to roughly eight to ten employees at a time so that no one becomes lost in the process of education. Trainees literally sit in a small circle. The trainer gets everyone involved in education by asking each person to make a contribution to the learning process. Trainers ask for trainees' opinions, ideas, and suggestions. Homework assignments can be a part of the learning process, and each participant can take turns leading the group the subsequent times the learning circle is held. Training is an ongoing process, and dozens of learning circles should be scheduled. You can use the Eight Components to guide your training and cover each component during one learning circle training session, for a total of eight learning circle sessions.

Gaining Support from Families and Other Professionals in the Community

Educating employees is only the beginning. Families and other professionals from the outside community will also require an understanding and appreciation of person-centered care. It is important to gain support and cooperation from family members and others from the very start and make them a part of the transition process. Families and other professionals, like medical directors and attending physicians, ombudsmen, outside therapy groups, and other ancillary staff, should take part in the design and implementation of person-centered care. Otherwise, they may not understand or appreciate it, may impede its development and progress, and may not accept all of the efforts you and your team are trying to achieve.

I recommend holding a special Family Night one evening where you introduce person-centered care to families, guardians, and others in the community. You can use the Eight Components to guide your presentation. In my experience, most families are absolutely delighted with what they hear at this meeting and are enthused about the changes that are going to take place. Most families are more than willing to participate in the process and become volunteers for the facility. One presentation will probably not be enough, so you may want to discuss progress briefly at future family meetings. You can also hold a special Town Hall meeting or a dinner for ancillary staff and physicians to introduce person-centered care. It has been my experience that physicians love to eat when there is a meeting, so make sure your kitchen prepares something delicious and exceptional for your doctors. They will love you for it!

Create a Person-Centered Care Committee and Vision Statement

Once you have introduced the idea of person-centered care to employees, residents, families, and other healthcare professionals, it is time to create a special committee that has the sole purpose of creating a new vision statement, outlining goals and objectives, spelling out core values, and setting the course for person-centered care. I am in debt to a wonderful long-term care administrator, Dionne Nicol, who has provided me with details concerning the development and execution of the person-centered care committee. She says, "The first step to culture change is sitting down with your team and creating a new vision for the facility."

The staff in one of her facilities, Crown Pointe Care Center in Columbus, Ohio, created a new vision statement for the kind of person-centered care they have adopted. It reads: "We are a community whose needs and wants are heard, understood, and met on an individual basis. We want you to be able to call Crown Pointe your home." The focus of their vision statement is on the resident's individual needs and unique wants as well as the creation of a place that feels like home.

The most important question to ask is, "What do we want our vision statement to say about our own brand of person-centered care in our facility?" A vision statement is necessary because it provides the driving force behind the committee's efforts to change the facility's culture. Dionne reminds us, "The administrator and director of nursing need to be willing to empower the staff to make changes in the facility. The chain of command should move away from the traditional bureaucratic pyramid to an upside-down pyramid, where the focus is not on management, but on everyone in the facility."

The steering committee is comprised of eight to ten employees from the facility. It is important to ask employees to volunteer for a position on the committee, which should represent management and floor staff equally. This is not a committee that is to be dominated by management. The ideas for change must come from everyone in the building, including residents and family members. You can simply send a voluntary sign-up form around the building to attract volunteers. The steering committee will meet and discuss various components of culture change that they want to see take place. The Eight Components can be used as a guide for steering committee meetings. Goals are set, timelines are created, and values are discussed at these meetings. The topics of person-centered care and culture change do not have to be isolated to just this committee, but should instead be discussed at resident and family council meetings and with the ombudsmen on a continuous basis.

Core Values and Principles

Beyond the mission statement, the steering committee can guide their work according to their own set of core values and principles. A good model of person-centered values and principles can be taken from the work of Thomas Kitwood. He provides a model of person-centered care that outlines the main psychological needs of the individual. These needs can become core values and principles that influence how person-centered care is developed and delivered in the facility. According to Kitwood, the ultimate psychological need is love (p. 81). This can be realized when the resident achieves a sense of comfort, attachment, inclusion, occupation, and identity. If we examine each psychological need as a core value or principle in person-centered care, we can work towards a new culture, one in which "love" is more important than "care," comfort is valued as much as safety, attachment and inclusion are answers to loneliness, and withdrawal, occupation, and identity are more important than treating every resident in the same manner.

Create a Culture of Compassion

Ultimately, the goal of the person-centered care committee, the new vision statement, and core values and principles that guide the committee are to create a "culture of compassion." This means that steps will be taken to move the facility away from an institution and towards a home where relationships and friendships are highly desired and valued.

The work of Brooker can be used to create a checklist or outline of necessary elements in a culture of compassion. She believes that a culture of compassion can be achieved through "positive person work," which involves seventeen aspects of care that are kind, considerate, and exceptional (pp. 90-95). The seventeen aspects of positive person work are:

1. Warmth—demonstrating genuine affection, care and concern,

2. Holding—providing safety, security, and comfort,

3. Relaxed Pace—creating a relaxing atmosphere,

4. Respect—treating residents as valued persons and recognizing their experience and age,

5. Acceptance—establishing relationships based on an attitude of acceptance and positive regard for the resident,

6. Celebration—recognizing, supporting, and taking delight in the abilities and skills of the resident,

7. Acknowledgment—recognizing, accepting, and supporting the resident as a unique person and valuing them as a real person,

8. Genuineness—maintaining an honest and open relationship with residents and being sensitive to their needs and feelings,

9. Validation—recognizing and supporting the reality of the resident's life; maintaining priority of their feelings and emotions,

10. Empowerment—letting go of control of the resident's life and activities; assisting the resident to participate in skills and abilities,

11. Facilitation—assessing the level of support required for the resident and providing it,

12. Enabling—recognizing and encouraging the resident's level of engagement in activities,

13. Collaboration—treating the resident like a partner, not a patient,

14. Recognition—appreciating the resident's uniqueness,

15. Including—enabling and encouraging the resident to be and feel included, physically and emotionally,

16. Belonging—providing a sense of acceptance regardless of the resident's abilities and disabilities, and

17. Fun—accessing a free, creative way of being; using and responding to fun and humor.

All seventeen aspects of positive person work can act as a framework for the person-centered care committee in setting goals, creating a vision, changing how care is thought about and delivered, and recreating their culture as a whole.

Getting Input from Residents and Families

Now that you have reviewed the Eight Components of person-centered care, introduced the idea to your staff and families and gained their support, developed a special committee and created a new vision statement, thought about and endorsed core values and principles, and are working towards a culture of compassion, it is time to get input from your residents and their families concerning what is important to them in terms of culture change. The best way to achieve this is to design surveys, questionnaires, or conduct interviews. The team can design any of these tools, and it may work best if each committee member assigns themselves between eight to ten residents to interview. The following questions can be helpful:

1. What are some of the major differences between living here and being home?

2. What would you like to see us do in the facility to make it feel more like home?

3. List and describe things that you don't like about the facility and the kind of care you receive.

4. When do you prefer to wake up in the morning and go to bed at night?

5. What are some of your favorite foods that we don't offer?

6. What are some of your favorite hobbies that you maintained at home but haven't kept up since you've moved here?

7. List and describe places that you've always enjoyed going to but haven't since you've moved here.

8. List and describe some things that would make you happier here.

After gathering all of the data you can from residents and family members, put it all together and analyze it qualitatively. Look for patterns and common themes in the data. What do your residents want most? Do they have issues with the design of the building or the quality of the food? Do they become bored with the same old activities month after month? Do they want a facility dog or cat? Do they wish they could get out more often and visit places in the community? Would they like to paint their room a different color or rearrange their furnishings?

It is important to gather this data and use it. Do not file it away after you and your team have collected it. This data should be the driving force in making changes in the facility towards a person-centered culture.

Whenever you are in doubt about making changes, ask the residents. Take this data and fit the resident's wishes and preferences into the Eight Components of person-centered care. Now, you are creating a model of care that is unique to your facility.

Adding It Up

This chapter provides a general framework for getting your person-centered care process started. It offers information on:

1. The Eight Components of person-centered care.

2. Presenting the idea to staff, families, and others in the community and gaining their support.

3. Developing a steering committee and creating a new person-centered care vision statement.

4. Determining core values and guiding principles of person-centered care and culture change.

5. Exploring elements in creating a culture of compassion.

6. Constructing a survey, questionnaire, or interview for residents and their families.

The next logical step is to take this information and start making changes in the facility. This can be challenging but also incredibly exciting. Use all of this information to help the steering committee identify areas in the facility requiring change now and in the near future. Take a critical look at the attitudes of your staff, the ways in which care is delivered, the use of personal and social space, the quality of food and dining services, the quality and meaningfulness of activities, the interaction between the facility and the outside community, and how leadership and management operate. Where will you start?

POINTS TO PONDER

1. Using the Eight Components of person-centered care as a guide, which area of your facility requires change the most?

2. How does your facility measure up in terms of the 17 aspects of positive person work and a culture of compassion?

3. What kinds of changes would your staff like to make in the facility? What kinds of changes would your residents want?

CHAPTER TWO: CULTURE CHANGE AND CREATING A HOME

Nothing can bring a real sense of security into the home except true love.

Billy Graham

Anyone who is talking about getting started or has already implemented components of person-centered care is ultimately attempting to change their facility's culture. The difference between the two is that person-centered care is, in my opinion, one of the most successful means of achieving significant and lasting changes in the culture of nursing homes. I have tied two important concepts together in this chapter—culture change and "home"—and for a good reason. The goal of changing a facility's culture through person-centered care is to move away from the traditional, institutional model of long-term care and move towards a dwelling or home. An essential point to remember when making cultural changes is to always rely on the information you've collected from your residents. This data should be the driving force behind modifications and alterations concerning how care is delivered, what kinds of foods are ordered, and how the physical environment is renovated. The goal is to make resident-directed changes, not staff-directed ones.

Defining and Understanding Culture Change

Culture change represents a paradigm shift from traditional and institutional long-term care to a person-centered home. Mitty defines this culture change as "a philosophy and a process that seeks to transform nursing homes from restrictive institutions to vibrant communities of older adults and the people who care for them" (p. 47). Empowering residents and employees to be self-determined decision makers and turning resident dependency and deterioration into growth, creativity, and regenerativity can lead to true culture change. Some authors (Tellis-Nayak, p. 22) view culture change as a call out to nursing homes across the nation to leave traditional long-term care culture behind and adopt one that is based on quality, affirmation, respect, choice, and empowerment.

In a sense, culture change is a choice by healthcare professionals to not simply redecorate their building and call it change, but instead to make deep changes in themselves concerning how they view quality of care and quality of life for those they serve. Culture change can also be viewed as a commitment to reinvent and reinvigorate their facility based on resident's desires, wishes, and preferences. Culture change can be considered an outcome of resident choice, but an outcome that is never quite fully achieved. It is an outcome that evolves and is reinvented over and over again to meet the needs of the residents living in their home. Some may wish to think of culture change as a journey from a highly institutionalized way of life to a more natural, spontaneous, and relaxed one.

The Meaning of Home

The boldest goal of culture change involves transforming the institution into a home. The idea of home is near and dear to all people in one way or another. Although it can have different meanings to different people, we can agree that home is a place of sanctuary and safety. It represents who we are as unique individuals and gives us a sense of pride and accomplishment. It is a place where we welcome family and friends. No matter how large or small, tidy or messy, we gain many psychological benefits from our home. Most of us have our own special places within our home, where we can escape and enjoy hobbies or activities that only we can appreciate. Home also provides privacy from the rest of the world, where we can be alone, share intimate relationships, celebrate, laugh, and cry, or just soak in the bathtub listening to jazz. We can be ourselves in the privacy of our own homes.

Unfortunately, there is a stark contrast between this description of home and life in a nursing home. Traditional long-term care places great emphasis on the building being a "facility" where employees work and which is owned by a corporation. It doesn't belong to the residents, but to some invisible owner who may or may not have ever set foot inside the building. Or, it may be perceived as a place that is operated and managed by employees. This is not to say that all traditional nursing homes can be characterized this way, but there are probably enough that are.

The larger point is that living in an institution is no way to live. Natural life is replaced by scheduled care, routines, and tasks that are performed on individuals. Living space is shared by roommates on a small scale, and dozens of other residents on a larger scale. Decisions concerning care are most times made by management or nursing staff. In many institutions, there is nowhere to go to be truly alone, nowhere to enjoy friends and family uninterrupted, and few private belongings that one can call his or her own. In other words, this is no home. In fact, nursing home residents could be considered homeless.

Explore and Scrutinize the Facility

One of the most practical ways of approaching changes in the facility is doing a walk-through with a pad of paper and pen, looking for every aspect you can find that is overly institutional. You can begin outside. Every home has a yard with plants, flowers, and trees. It also has a front door, mailbox, and address on it. Entering through the front door should be delightful—not frightful. What do you smell? Sugar cookies baking or disinfectant floor soap? Even worse—do you smell urine? Some facilities that I work with have decided to use cookie ovens, popcorn machines, elaborate coffee machines, or crock pots of fresh soup in various areas of the building, including the receptionist area, front offices, or on each unit. The benefit is a comforting olfactory experience—it smells like home.

Are manager's offices far-removed from where residents live? Do the offices take up a lot of space? This is space that residents could use. Another facility I work with remodeled a room that wasn't being used and turned it into a café, complete with fresh coffee, popcorn, cookies, books, magazines, and Internet access. Resident, families and staff all use it and love it. As you make your way around the building, be sure to jot down what you see and what it could become with some creativity and imagination—just make sure it's what the residents want.

As you get deeper into the heart of the facility, are there large, bulky nurses' stations on each unit? Many facilities engaged in person-centered care and culture change are eliminating them and no longer find any good use for them. Do your nurses still pass meds with their large, institutional-looking med carts? I don't have a nurses' station or med cart in my house, do you? Remember—you are trying to remove things that look institutional and to make the place more of a home or a house. A facility that I work with removed a nurses' station and created a warm and inviting living space for the residents. It consisted of a working fireplace, a large flat screen television, comfortable chairs and couches, a built-in library wall, and an Internet work station. Which would you rather have in your facility?

Take a walk through your dining rooms. Most are large because we believed larger was better for residents and staff. The current thought about this is that smaller, cozier, and more intimate spaces are better because they are not over-stimulating, noisy, and bright. I would imagine that residents diagnosed with dementia would manage better in a smaller dining room. Most facilities use four-top tables, and they all are identical. It is certainly easier to order tables in bulk and create a uniform look throughout not only the dining room, but the entire facility. Although the tables can be very nice, they tend to create an institutional feel—almost like a hospital. Larger dining rooms are being replaced by smaller dining rooms, and dining room tables that seat eight or more people are replacing four-top tables. A dining room table symbolizes family, comfort, good food, and home.

Walking through your facility with a new set of eyes, through a new "cultural lens" if you will, can be very revealing. I will discuss more physical and environmental changes that can be made in the building later. I don't want to create the impression that culture change involves redecorating your facility and that's it—because it involves so much more than that. What it relies on most is resident choice.

The Importance of Resident Choice

After you and your staff walk through the building and evaluate what changes should be made, go back to the resident data that you collected. Compare your recommendations to the preferences, choices, and ideas voiced by your residents. Although there will be some similarities and some differences, use your resident data as your compass in deciding which changes are most important to them. This is not to say that you and your staff have no voice at all—indeed you do. But when in doubt, stay resident-centered—it's their house.

If we are to truly fulfill resident choice and preference, we should try to honor their decisions as much as possible. Perhaps every resident room in the facility is painted beige and a particular resident doesn't care for that color. They would prefer to have their room painted canary yellow. What now? If you truly want to be a person-centered home, you paint the room canary yellow. Each room in our home is not the same color, but instead each is either painted or papered according to our taste, mood, and unique style. We must make strong efforts to give our residents an active voice in their care and how they want to live their life. We must be committed to maximizing independence and autonomy, not just in theory, but in reality. This may involve allowing some residents to wake up at 10:00 a.m. and eat breakfast in their pajamas in the dining room. I eat breakfast at 10:00 a.m. sometimes and usually in night clothes, so why can't they?

An important element in person-centered care or culture change involves providing the means for residents to express their identity, culture, race, gender, and religion. This can be achieved in a number of ways, including menu changes reflecting various ethnic food offerings, different types of recreation and activities, and personal lifestyle choices. You should learn quite a bit about your residents by interviewing them and collecting data that reflect such preferences. You and the direct care staff can learn their likes and dislikes, their preferences, and their daily routines.

It is important to know at what time residents prefer to wake up in the morning, what kinds of food they like for breakfast, lunch, and dinner, whether they like to be showered before or after meals, whether they like to be dressed or in night clothes for breakfast, and whether they like to watch television, listen to the radio, or read the newspaper during their meals. If the resident is unable to communicate his or her preferences, ask family members. If there are no surviving family members, rely on nursing assistants who have worked closely with the resident. Our nursing assistants know a lot about residents, and sometimes we take this for granted. The point is to become aware of what residents want and put their desires into action.

Dealing Effectively with Resistance to Change

Changes do not take place without challenges. It is human nature for some people to resist change, fear it, or demand that things remain the same. I have seen various reactions from staff concerning the implementation of person-centered care in their building. While most were thrilled about it and welcomed it with open arms, there were those who didn't believe it would work, thought it would cost too much, believed it to be a fad, or did not want to deviate from "the ways things have always been done around here." Since I've encountered some resistance to change, I've decided to interview staff and ask them what it is they fear. Some of their concerns were as follows:

1. They weren't sure if state regulations allowed for all of the changes that management was talking about making.

2. They weren't sure how person-centered care would change the care plans.

3. They were fearful that their jobs would become tougher and they would have to take on more roles.

4. The thought of allowing certain residents to make their own decisions frightened them.

5. They felt that they were losing control as employees.

6. They saw person-centered care as creating more work for them, yet they were not receiving a raise for it.

7. They were nervous about certain families not accepting person-centered care and creating problems.

8. They thought some staff may misuse person-centered care and instead of trying to get a resident to eat, wake up, or cooperate with care, they could easily say, "It's their choice. Leave them alone."

The best way to deal with resistance, in my opinion, is to allow staff to express their concerns and anxieties about change and address them as genuinely as possible. This means that there is no need to sugarcoat the situation. Culture change takes time, patience, commitment, and hard work. Even after this, it is never quite done. Focus on the benefits of person-centered care, not only to residents, but to employees as well. Encourage them to be a partner in recreating the culture of the home and emphasize how important they are in the process. Each employee brings a distinctive energy and personality, and they are vital in the making of a new culture of care.

Adding It Up

True culture change involves an ideological shift from treating residents in an institution to providing them with quality of life in their home. Most individuals want a place that they can call their home, and being admitted into a nursing home is no reason to abandon this desire. After reading this chapter, take a good, hard look at your facility. Ask yourself, "Does it remind me more of a traditional medical institution or more of a comfortable and happy home?" In an institution, choices are made by the staff, and in one's home, individuals make their own choices. Choice is important, and residents should be able to make as many choices as their physical and cognitive status allows them to make about their care and lifestyle. Employees will respond to change in various ways—some will welcome it while others may fear or resist it. Deal with emotional reactions to culture change and creating a home for your residents immediately. Handle your employee reactions in a genuine and caring way. Open up lines of communication, build trust, and help your employees move forward, reminding them each step of the way that they are doing something incredible and honorable for the people whom they serve.

POINTS TO PONDER

1. How would you describe your facility's current culture? Is it more institutional or home-like?

2. After taking a walk through your facility, what kinds of changes would you make to create a greater sense of home?

3. Do your residents make most of their own choices concerning meals, activities, and their personal schedule or do your employees make more decisions for them?

CHAPTER THREE:
THE IMPORTANCE OF FOOD
AND THE DINING EXPERIENCE

There is no love sincerer than the love of food.

George Bernard Shaw

There perhaps is no better place to make significant changes in long-term care than in dietary services. Many facilities implementing person-centered care choose to make dietary changes first because food is important to everyone. When there are improvements in food, people notice.

The importance of food has been well documented throughout human history. Hippocrates made the connection between food and health over two thousand years ago when he said, "Let food be your medicine." Food not only nourishes the body, it has the power to heal and comfort people. It is a symbol of nurturing, love, and celebration. Meals are many times the high point of the residents' day.

Although food itself is of great importance in long-term care, the dining experience must be inviting and attentive to the needs of the residents. How food is prepared, presented, and served all impact the dining experience. Food should be attractive and desired. If no one eats, it has no value to anyone. Unfortunately a fair amount of food is wasted on a daily basis in nursing homes. Nothing says "the food around here stinks" more than when it ends up in the garbage. Not only is this an unfortunate waste in general, but dietary services must feel terrible about the amount of food that is thrown away. Dietary services, in my opinion, have been underappreciated for years in long-term care facilities. Now is the time for dieticians, chefs, dietary managers, and kitchen staff to let their creativity flow.

What's Wrong with Food in Long-Term Care?

What kinds of changes should you make in dietary services? There are a few important questions to ask. First, what do your residents want to eat? Are they choosing what ends up on the menu, or does the dietary manager make all of the ordering decisions? Elderly individuals living in long-term care facilities have life-long patterns of food and dining preferences and expectations. An essential feature of person-centered care involves residents making their own food choices. Second, where do they have their meals? Do they have choices in where they eat? Are meals served in one large dining area, or in several smaller dining rooms? Are these areas brightly lit, noisy, crowded, and over-stimulating? Is there more focus on getting meals out on time or on customer service and an ideal dining experience? Third, what are meals being served on? Faded plastic plates, bowls, and coffee cups, or fine china? Are deserts being served in Styrofoam containers or glass stemware? Are milk and juice served in cartons or glasses? Are you still serving food on trays? I believe that tray service is becoming a thing of the past. I haven't eaten off of a tray since high school and have no plan to start now. Lastly, when do residents prefer having their meals? When the facility says so or when they prefer to eat? Is there any flexibility in dining hours, or are all meals served according to a rigid schedule? If they sleep in late can they still order breakfast at 9:30 a.m.?

Without running the risk of sounding too negative, food in many long-term care facilities can be greatly improved. Elderly people living in long-term care facilities already run a higher risk of malnutrition or under-nutrition, so it is critical that the kitchen serves food that residents want, where they want it, and in a way that enhances the dining experience. Based on my observations and interviews with residents, some of the most common complaints about food include the following: it's not what they want to eat, it's bland, colorless, not served at appropriate temperatures, it's always the same, it lacks creativity, and there is little joy in eating. It's no wonder that "unintended" weight loss occurs, that pressure ulcers and infections develop, and anemia, hypotension, and bone fractures are problematic in long-term care—they are all associated with nutritional status.

Innovative Changes in Dietary Services

Purchasing foods requested by residents is only part of the solution in improving dining services. The other part involves how food is delivered, served and accessed. I have worked with facilities that have made many changes in their kitchen, and the results have been phenomenal. The following changes discussed in this chapter are fresh and imaginative. They are all good ways of raising the bar on quality. Among the dietary changes I have seen in the field and throughout the most current literature on person-centered care, I believe that eight of them deserve individual attention. Buffets, restaurant-style dining, fine dining, home-style dining, room service, 24-hour dining, drive-through dining, and the use of kitchenettes have proven to be very successful.

Buffett Dining

A great way of presenting and serving food for breakfast, lunch, and dinner involves a real crowd-pleaser: the buffet. We have all eaten from buffets during the course of our lives and in my opinion, many elderly people enjoy them. One of my fondest memories of Mother's Day is being a young teen and going out with the entire family to a popular local restaurant that had a huge and marvelous brunch buffet. They offer variety and choice, and foods are served fresh and at appropriate temperatures. Everyone can benefit from buffet-style dining. Most ambulatory residents can walk through the buffet line and serve themselves, and those in wheelchairs or who require assistance can go through the buffet with the help of staff.

The breakfast buffet can be set up each morning on every unit, hall, or floor, depending on how your facility is designed. You may want to start slowly and offer the breakfast buffet once a week until your staff and residents get used to it. Eggs, hash browns, bacon, toast, fruit, cereals, coffee, milk, juice, and teas can be featured on the buffet. You can change the items weekly, monthly, or quarterly—remember it's up to your residents what kinds of food end up on the buffet. For lunch, the buffet can serve sandwiches, soup, and salad. The dinner buffet can offer the heartiest foods of the day, like meat loaf, mashed potatoes, vegetables, breads, deserts, and drinks.

Some benefits of buffet-style dining include the obvious, such as variety and choice, but residents will choose only the items they want and the waste should be very minimal. I have seen some elderly residents ask for one egg, two pieces of bacon, and toast for breakfast and others who simply want a bowl of oatmeal. Buffets can offer an alternative to traditional tray service for any meal of the day. A good portion of food on trays often ends up in the trash. In some facilities, employees sit and eat breakfast, lunch, and dinner with their residents. This is a very refreshing part of culture change that brings employees and residents together.

Residents eat what they want, share meals with their caregivers, and enjoy life at a normal pace.

Restaurant-Style Dining

Although I have read about restaurant-style dining and heard of facilities that tried it, I became truly excited when I sat down with two professionals and discussed what they were doing and then saw it with my own eyes. Mark Grippi, LNHA, and Chef Will Rosch of Beachwood Pointe in Beachwood, Ohio, decided that they would offer their residents an enjoyable restaurant experience complete with a hostess, white linens, china and glassware, kitchen staff dressed in chef's coats, menus on every table, and waiters and waitresses taking their orders. Chef Will told me that before they implemented restaurant-style dining, less than half of the dining room would be full for any meal. After they rolled it out, there is barely a seat left. The benefits of this dining style include increased appetite and food consumption, socialization, and development of relationships. It is a familiar way for adults to experience meals. Residents order a la carte from menus, and while waiting for the main course, staff offer bread, soup, salad, and drinks.

Fine Dining

One way to raise the bar in dietary services is to offer a fine dining experience once a week or month. Fine dining is closely related to restaurant-style dining, except that the menu offers high-end foods such as filet mignon, crab cakes, lobster bisque, shrimp cocktail, elaborate side dishes, decadent deserts, and wine. The environment can be enhanced and ambiance created by the use of candles and fresh flowers on each table, and jazz music in the dining room. The goal for dietary staff is to create a relaxing 5-star dining experience for residents.

Home Style Dining

One of the most comforting memories for elderly residents is their family gathering around the kitchen or dining room table and sharing a family meal. This experience from their past can be recreated in the facility with a little creativity and desire from the staff. I have personally found that home style dining works best in facilities that have broken down large hallways into smaller and more manageable neighborhoods. Within such an environment, one caregiver and seven or eight residents can share a meal that is prepared in the kitchen and brought to the dining room table in their own neighborhood.

Serving home style meals is easy and involves foods that can be prepared in large casseroles, crock pots, and serving dishes. A typical meal can include lasagna, tossed salad, and a loaf of garlic bread, served directly from the pans and bowls on the table. Just like in your home or mine, family members scoop out their own food portions and go back for seconds as they please. Residents who require assistance can gain all of the benefits of eating with their caregiver and friends with a little help. Sundays during football season can be very enriching as the group eats in front of the big screen television—just like home.

Room Service

Although most facilities offer meals in the resident's room, it can hardly compare to receiving 5-star room service like one would receive in a full-service hotel. Room service is a nice amenity that most of us enjoy. We have many expectations concerning room service, including exceptional customer service, friendly and timely service, fresh, well-prepared food, and a flower on the cart delivered to our room. Why can't we provide this same level of service in long-term care facilities? In my opinion, there is no reason not to. The idea of room service is much more pleasant that simply eating in one's room. Room service is provided when it is requested. Many elderly people enjoy eating their meals in front of the television in their room or while talking to family members on the phone. So, why not let them? This type of service can bring normalcy to their lives and make them feel more at home.

24-Hour Dining

When I bring up 24-hour dining to some health-care professionals, they look at me as if I am speaking complete gibberish. "How do you expect to offer meals twenty-four hours a day in a nursing home?" they ask. It's rather easy! The kitchen prepares meals as they normally would, plating the protein, carbohydrate, and vegetable complete with garnish. They will make a few extra plates and store them in the refrigerator. If a resident misses a meal due to an appointment or is too ill to eat during a meal time, he or she can have the same meal they missed. All staff must do is remove it from the refrigerator and microwave it. And there you have it—a fresh, hot meal served just as it would be during meal times. This, in my opinion, is much better than a pack of cookies, crackers, or peanut butter and jelly sandwiches as a meal substitute.

Drive-Through Dining

I receive equally blank stares from some employees when I discuss one of the most creative dining styles I have seen in person-centered care facilities—the drive-through service. I want to give full credit where credit is due. This idea came from a fantastically imaginative director of quality of life (activities) at a long-term care facility in Olmsted Falls, Ohio. Her name is Terry Willingham, ADC, and when I first met her I thought to myself, *This is either one of the most ingenious activity directors I have ever met or she is completely off her rocker!* I have since made up my mind that she is both. She takes some of the craziest ideas and turns them into fun and exciting activities.

Terry's facility has a general store in the front entrance, and they use it for all sorts of activities—including a fast-food, drive-through window! Terry told me that on Fridays, the drive-through serves fish-n-chips, burgers and fries, or hot dogs. Everyone in the building knows that lunch will be at the drive-through.

Residents and their families as well as staff all go through the drive-through and order their food. Residents in wheelchairs also make their way through the line and get their food. This is an original idea, but the real benefit is that everyone loves it and gets a real kick out of it. It brings fun to the facility.

Kitchenettes

One way to ensure that food is available twenty-four hours a day is to build small kitchenettes in each hallway, unit or neighborhood. This concept includes the availability of a small refrigerator, microwave, hot plate or plug-in grill, and coffee pot. Cabinets can be stocked with microwave soups, frozen dinners, pancake mix, pretzels, potato chips, popcorn, bread, cereals, and hot chocolate. The refrigerator can be stocked with yogurts, fruit, puddings, milk, juice, deli meats and cheeses, and other foods that residents want to eat. Our kitchen is never closed in our own homes, why should it be closed after certain hours in long-term care? The use of small kitchenettes eliminates the problem of the closed kitchen. Residents, their families, and staff can take a peek in the kitchenette whenever they wish and have a small meal or snack at any time through the day or night—just like at home.

The Importance of Comfort Foods in Long-Term Care

In an effort to improve not only quality of nutrition but quality of life, dietary departments can introduce into the menu and at the direction of residents more comfort foods. Why comfort foods? Why not comfort foods! Everyone loves eating foods that make us feel good inside. We all have memories of mom (or dad!) baking apple pies, sugar cookies, cakes, roasts, turkey, chili, and pasta. The aroma alone from these foods can elevate our mood and bring us great comfort. Psychologically speaking, this is a no-brainer. Comfort foods can create a wide number of benefits to elderly and medically frail individuals who sometimes are looking for comfort wherever they can find it. Comfort foods can also bring back wonderful memories of childhood and youth.

There are various types of comfort foods including nostalgic foods, indulgence foods, convenience foods, and physical comfort foods (Locher, et al., p. 273). They are meant to enhance an individual's sense of well-being and provide short-term relief from stress. Some people turn to comfort foods for security or reward. Many comfort foods simply make us happy. When we are children, we usually go after foods like potato chips, ice cream, candy, and chocolate. Anything baked by our parents such as birthday cakes, chocolate chip cookies, or homemade pies can bring back wonderful memories and give us a sense of continuity and joy. As children, we also enjoy heavy carbohydrates such as mac-n-cheese, pizza, French fries or tater tots, grilled cheese sandwiches and fish sticks. As we get a little older, our tastes change and we start to enjoy heavier-tasting foods including pasta, tacos, burgers, and many other fast-food varieties. Later in life as adults, we turn to hearty but healthier foods such as sea food, soups and salads, chicken and beef dishes, and potatoes.

There are some important elements to making comfort foods. First, the secret to creating a good comfort food is by using two main ingredients: complex carbohydrates (sugar, refined wheat, and rice) and fat. We all know that everything is better with bacon, and when dietary introduces a little bacon fat in a recipe it is sure to be a hit. Second, comfort food should be something that is considered "home cooking" or made from scratch in the kitchen. Southern fried chicken appropriately fits this description, and who would not enjoy the aroma of deep fried chicken in their facility? The last element is affordability—comfort foods do not have to break the dietary budget. As a matter of fact, they are fairly inexpensive compared to other kinds of processed and prepared foods.

Benefits of comfort foods can be physical, social, and psychological. They can stimulate one's appetite, maintain a healthy weight, and keep an aging body in good health. Eating such foods can increase cognition and mental alertness, improve energy level and stamina, and can aid in wound healing. Socially, comfort foods bring people together and give residents something to look forward to. They can stimulate memories from the past and give residents something to talk about. Psychologically and emotionally, comfort foods can bring back feelings of home, family, holidays, and special events. Certain foods can improve mood, decrease depression and anxiety, and give residents a sense of calm and pleasure.

Practically speaking, you need to find out what kinds of comfort foods your residents would enjoy most and get them on the menu. Offering a hot (or cold) cup of soup before lunch or dinner is a nice place to start. Bread and butter on every table is another simple solution in providing more comfort foods. Soups and breads can be made from scratch in the kitchen or with the assistance of residents who want to share their recipes. I am sure there are residents out there who have some great chicken noodle soup, chili, or Old World European bread recipes. Sharing these recipes can also give residents a great sense of purpose and meaning.

Sandwiches are simple and provide another good way to provide comfort foods to residents. BLTs, the classic grilled cheese, ham and cheese, pastrami, the Reuben, and other deli-style sandwiches offer nutrition and comfort. Open faced beef or turkey sandwiches can be real crowd pleasers during cooler seasons. Remember that many elderly people grew up eating at diners throughout the country, and they will enjoy foods that remind them of old fashioned diner-style meals that they enjoyed long ago. Some good side dishes include potato, egg and macaroni salads, coleslaw, and baked beans. Main course dishes can include beef stew, meatloaf, burgers, Salisbury steak, roasted chicken or turkey, and baked ham. The potato is a wonderful comfort food and the possibilities are endless. Whether they are fried, mashed, baked, scalloped, or roasted, most people love potatoes. The end of a great comforting meal is undoubtedly a fantastic dessert. "Life is unpredictable—eat dessert first!" Most if not all desserts should be made from scratch in the kitchen. Homemade cakes, pies, cookies, puddings, cobblers, tarts, tortes, and strudels can put the final touches on a wonderful meal. I spoke to a dietary manager not too long ago, and he told me that of all the desserts that he creates, his residents love pie every single day. A day should not go by without pie. His particular group of residents must have grown up enjoying pie, and that shouldn't be a problem now that they are in a nursing home. Person-centered care is about resident choice, so if they want pie, give them pie! Old-fashioned and homemade ice cream, mousse, custard, and fresh fruit desserts can also be a real hit after a satisfying meal.

Extended Meals Times

A principal feature of person-centered care and culture change is flexibility in almost every aspect of living, including when meals are served and for how long they are served. Extended meal times offer residents a wider timeframe for each meal: breakfast, lunch, and dinner. More time means that residents do not have to conform to the facility's schedule for meals. It also gives residents the opportunity to sleep in later in the morning, take an extra-long nap in the afternoon and enjoy a later supper rather than an early dinner. I have worked with facilities that have extended their meal times as follows: breakfast is held between 7:00 a.m. and 9:30 a.m.; lunch is served between 11:30 a.m. and 1:30 p.m. and dinner is served between 4:30 p.m. to 7:00 p.m. Does this make things tougher in the kitchen? No! It actually gives dietary staff more time to focus on quality instead of dishing out food within a small amount of time.

Extended meals give residents opportunities that they would not otherwise have, including waking up late and making their way to the breakfast buffet in their pajamas at 9:00 a.m. Perhaps they have guests coming in from out of town who will not arrive until 7:00 p.m. With flexible meal times, this is no problem. The resident and his or her guests will receive a full meal and dessert shortly after 7:00 p.m., just as they would if they were still at home. Some residents are early risers and others are night owls. Why should they change their lifelong patterns to fit the institutional mold? When residents are given choice to eat when they want, they may eat more, receive better nutritional value, and benefit physically and psychologically.

The Liberalized Diet

The following information is directly from the American Dietetic Association (2005), which maintains the position that "the quality of life and nutritional status of older residents in long-term care facilities may be enhanced by liberalization of the diet prescription" (p. 1316). Although this information has been available since 2005,

I am always amazed to discover how many long-term care professionals aren't familiar with it. In my opinion, the liberalized diet essentially means that if you are old, sick, or frail and live in a nursing home, eat whatever you want, whenever you want it, and forget about portions! I realize that common sense must prevail, but food is one of the last pleasures for many residents. Why approach eating so scientifically?

The liberalized diet is concerned with maintenance of health and the promotion of quality of living. Dietary departments can create healthy dishes that are tasty and satisfying. Food should be made that residents want to eat. Dieticians, chefs, dietary managers, and kitchen staff should keep an open mind concerning person-centered dining and weigh out the benefits and risks of offering certain foods. One thing is certain, institutional food services don't work well in long-term care and should be changed. Malnutrition, dehydration, pressure sores, infections, anemia, fractures, confusion, and impaired cognition can all be associated with diet, so liberalizing what residents eat is critical for physiological reasons.

The American Dietetic Association believes that residents should choose what they eat and that their ethnicity and cultural background should be taken into consideration by dietary services. Diversity in meals can be very exciting, while tasteless institutional food is usually boring and left uneaten. Food choices are important, and if residents feel they have no control over what they eat, this can be psychologically damaging and lead to withdrawal, loss of autonomy, and poor self-esteem. Institutional diets that are low in cholesterol, fat, and sugar are simply no fun for anyone and may take the joy out of eating.

The kitchen must be well-staffed to roll out person-centered dining and the liberalized diet. It would be difficult to provide a high quality dining experience with a skeleton crew. Also of great importance is the attitude of the staff toward the food they serve. What does your staff say about your facility's food? Do they eat it as often as they can, or do they avoid it? The attitudes of the staff usually influence the attitudes of residents.

What about residents diagnosed with diabetes? Can they eat whatever they want? The American Dietetic Association states, "The imposition of dietary restrictions on elderly residents with diabetes in long-term health facilities is not warranted," and "There is no evidence to support 'no concentrated sweets' or 'no sugar added' diets. It is preferable to make medication changes rather than implement food restrictions to control the blood glucose" (p. 1320). I have always felt that offering a big piece of chocolate cake to non-diabetic residents and giving those with diabetes a colorless, tasteless glob of sugar-free gelatin is a form of torture. Especially when the diabetic resident watches the others have their cake and eat it, too. Somehow, I felt this to be unfair. My argument has always been this: if I want a piece of cake after dinner tonight and I am diabetic, I will check my insulin and adjust it accordingly. In nursing homes, we surely have enough nurses to handle this, don't we? Why so strict? There is no longer any reason to be.

The dietician and dietary manager are critical members of the team and must decide which residents in the facility can benefit from the liberalized diet and those who may be at risk. After assessing the situation, you may discover that the vast majority of residents in your facility can enjoy a liberalized diet. Care plans must still be developed and the resident's nutritional status and medical conditions must be taken into consideration. The residents' personal food preferences must also be taken into account. The American Dietetic Association believes that "a liberalized approach to diet prescriptions, when appropriate, can enhance both quality of life and nutritional status" (p. 1316).

Food and Dementia

Person-centered dining and the liberalized diet should not be provided exclusively for populations of residents who are not diagnosed with a cognitive disorder such as Alzheimer's disease or dementia. Some healthcare professionals may worry about safety issues surrounding buffet dining or kitchenettes. "Won't demented residents stick their hands in the buffet?" "I'm worried they will put their hands on a hot pot of coffee or misuse the microwave." Here's my answer: "Then help them!" Confused residents should be safe and well supervised by employees anyway, so I don't see any problem with upgrading their environment and improving their quality of life through person-centered measures. We must still exercise common sense! The buffet should be monitored and operated by kitchen staff and a nursing assistant or nurse should be in the dining room during meals. Don't fall into a common trap that many facilities have. They will find more reasons why they can't provide person-centered care than reasons to support it. This is why creativity and teamwork are essential in culture change.

Some simple ideas for offering food on dementia units (by the way, I would like to see most units open, but that is a topic for another book!) is to offer residents finger foods throughout the day. Some residents forget how to perform simple functions like using eating utensils, so this can be particularly beneficial for them. Residents can maintain dignity and independence to some degree by eating finger foods such as apple slices, sandwiches, carrots, burgers, hot dogs, chicken nuggets, cookies, and pretzels. These items will have to be monitored, but they can add to the food service provided on special units. If weight loss is an issue, this may be one practical way to improve it. If confused residents are not complying with rigid meal schedules, this may also help. The point is to offer small amounts of food throughout the day and evening and give confused residents a choice in what they want to eat and when they want to eat it. This kind of flexibility can also improve behaviors or decrease negatives ones, such as combativeness or aggressiveness. Residents living on special units should still have choice and normalcy, and this is just one way to provide it.

The Resident-Directed Menu

Two innovative healthcare professionals, Mark Grippi, LNHA, and Chef Will, both of Beachwood Pointe Care Center in Beachwood, Ohio, developed what they call the "resident-directed menu." They are the only ones using it of whom I am aware.

What is the resident-directed menu? It is exactly what it sounds like—residents choose the foods from vendor catalogues and the dietary manager or chef orders them—period. Mark and Chef Will started out by interviewing residents concerning their food likes and dislikes, discussed food at resident council meetings, and then formed a special food committee. I remember Mark once telling me "You know, we have been ordering food for residents for years based on what we think they want, but no one has really never asked them—how silly is that?" I couldn't agree more!

The resident-directed menu has been a huge success. Residents eat more, enjoy their food, the dining room is full, and "eating" has become "dining." Residents socialize more and moods have improved. Chef Will even invites residents into the kitchen and asks them to share their favorite recipes with him. They make new dishes together and then serve them to the whole house. How radical is that? It is incredible in my opinion!

Adding It Up

Food and dining are very important to all of us, and they are surely highlights of the day for many residents in long-term care. Great improvements can be made in every dietary department across the country. The time is now to turn your food service into person-centered dining.

Here are some final things to think about when making changes in dietary. Provide a room for residents and families to dine privately. Make sure it is inviting and comfortable. Many special occasions can be held there. The main dining room is probably large and can be overwhelming to many residents, particularly those who are confused. Find ways to make the room "smaller" by creating partitions, redecorating, or re-arranging furniture. If it is in your budget to buy new tables, think about purchasing traditional dining room tables instead of the institutional 4-top tables. Use fewer florescent lights and more natural lighting where possible. Put salt and pepper, sugar, hot sauce, and other condiments on tables. Get rid of tray lines as soon as possible. They are becoming a thing of the past. Make as much as you can from scratch in the kitchen including desserts and soups. The kitchen should be the heart of the facility, so try to put food services as close to residents as possible. There is a big difference between frying bacon where everyone can smell it and it being prepared far away from residents and being delivered lukewarm on a plate. Finally, remember to always consult long-term care regulations and fire codes when thinking of new ideas.

POINTS TO PONDER

1. How would you describe the quality of food served in your facility?

2. Are you satisfied with how food is served to residents or can service be improved? How?

3. If you were to make changes in your facility's food services, where would you start?

4. Does your facility have a resident-directed food committee?

CHAPTER FOUR:
ACTIVITIES AND QUALITY
OF LIFE

It is a happy talent to know how to play.

Ralph Waldo Emerson

What do residents of long-term care facilities want most from the activity department? They want exciting activities that provide them with purpose, significance, and meaning. Is this easier said than done, unrealistic, idealistic, or an unachievable goal? No! Today's activity professional can lead the way in culture change by taking activities to a whole new level. Providing activities with purpose can give more meaning to life, because they offer something to look forward to today, tomorrow, and next month.

Quality of Care vs. Quality of Life

A great place to start in discussing activities that provide purpose is to examine the differences between quality of care and quality of life. It may be safe to say

---

that most long-term care facilities both understand and deliver good quality of care. Despite this, one area of long-term care that can be improved through purposeful activities is quality of life.

On one hand, quality of care involves the delivery of nursing care, physician services, and occupational, physical, and speech therapy. Care involves direct treatment from clinical staff including the distribution of medication, treatment of wounds and pressure sores, and trachea and vent maintenance. On the other hand, quality of life involves so much more—all of the other things that provide meaning, purpose, and significance in one's life.

Residents in long-term care can find great quality of life from activities, events, and outings sponsored by the activity department. Quality of life also involves enjoying delicious foods and beverages, wonderful customer service, and in particular, first-class dining services. Who in long-term care would not enjoy receiving company from friends, family, and neighbors? It may not be the number of people that one has in his or her life that brings about good quality of life, but the quality of relationships that may lead to greater quality of life.

Quality of life may be achieved through the element of daily surprises from the activities department. Spontaneous parties and celebrations could bring real joy to long-term care residents, who may have become used to an institutional way of life. Quality of life may also be found outside of the facility's walls—in the community. Many people have the need to belong to something larger and greater than themselves. One way of achieving this feeling is to belong to the community in which we live. We can also bring quality of life to our residents through good, old fashioned, tender loving care, respect, and dignity. And last, we can provide great quality of life by bringing as much "home" we can into the facility. Nothing says "quality of life" like living in our own home.

Why Is Quality of Life So Important?

Think of yourself as an elderly resident living in a long-term care facility. What would you need to achieve a high quality of life or at minimum, a high quality short-term stay? Some of you may need wireless Internet, books, magazines, and music. Others may say they need a high definition, flat-screen television with a wide choice of cable channels. Still others may say that they would require great food, fine dining, adult beverages, and access to food all of the time. Regardless of what you may need, quality of life is essential to living with purpose. Quality of life is highly associated with many other important factors, such as life satisfaction, physical and psychological health and well-being, and happiness. Quality of life relies on one's ability to actually get what one wants out of life. It is based on our achievements throughout our lifetime. It is also associated with our ability to continue to be important to other people and to contribute to our environment. It is tied to our ability to be a part of something much bigger than ourselves.

Activities and Quality of Life: What's the Connection?

Who better to provide fun and meaningful activities, events, community outings, great food, wonderful customer service, daily surprises, genuine relationships, and a sense of home than the activity professional? Above everything else necessary in long-term care—beyond state regulations, beyond staff and scheduling issues, and beyond the necessary paperwork—delivering as much quality of life to residents as possible is today's activity professional's first and most important goal. Who else in long-term care can create events and opportunities in which residents are recognized for who they really are? Who better to collaborate with residents on a daily basis in determining what activities and programs get scheduled in the building? Is it not the activity professional who is the life of the facility? Of course it is! Today's activity professional can bring a great deal of quality to residents' lives through play, celebration, validation, and sometimes just plain old goofing off.

The types of activities that may bring great quality to the lives of our residents are those that simply make them happy. People in general prefer doing things that bring them joy, and they retract from things that make them feel uncomfortable. Residents may also prefer activities that give them a sense of accomplishment and pride. These may involve cognitive and educational challenges or hobbies and crafts that take a long time to accomplish (i.e., model airplanes, certificate degrees online). Residents may intuitively wish to attend activities that make sense to them—in other words they find value in the activity or event that is scheduled. If it makes no sense, a resident may be a "no-show." They want something to look forward to both in the short- and long-term. If the activity professional can find something that most residents love to do, become excited about, and greatly anticipate, he or she has done something wonderful in their facility— provided activities with purpose.

Activities and Personhood

Hobbies, leisure, personal interests, and entertainment all reflect something unique and original about each individual. Each one of us enjoys our own kind of music, movies, fiction and non-fiction, sports, and other interests. Each of these plays a big part in what can be called our "personhood." Dr. Thomas Kitwood stressed the importance of personhood in his book *Dementia Reconsidered: The Person Comes First* (p. 8). He believes that maintaining personhood is one of the most important goals for caregivers, especially when the individual is diagnosed with dementia. This can be accomplished by providing physical care, exercising resident choice, and encouraging residents to use their abilities and express their feelings. It also involves developing and maintaining healthy relationships. Personhood can also be achieved through carefully designed activities that provide social attention, personal support, and the ability to exercise personal choice and decision-making. Activities can provide great psychosocial and emotional benefits to residents and can also boost self-esteem and confidence as well as joy in life.

Activities and Personal Growth

Activities that allow for and encourage personal growth are truly person-centered activities. Small discussion groups led by the activities director or an assistant can be very fulfilling to everyone involved. Sharing personal stories and biographies can be fun and informative. This also provides opportunity for residents to get to know each other and form deeper relationships. When residents tell their life stories, they are sharing their identity with others. This type of activity also preserves and enhances personhood. Individuals diagnosed with dementia can still engage in this type of activity with the assistance of props and cues such as music and movies from their era, photographs of themselves and their families, and anything else that will trigger memories of days gone by. Try not to underestimate what residents with dementia will and will not remember. They may surprise you!

Types of Activities: Restful, Active, Unscheduled, Ongoing, and Spontaneous

All activity directors know exactly what kinds of activities "should" be provided according to the regulations. They are restful, active, unscheduled, and ongoing. A new person-centered activity is called the "spontaneous activity," and this type of activity holds a great deal of promise for increasing quality of life, meaning and purpose in the lives of residents. I do not want to encourage you to stray away from traditional activities, because they are necessary and can provide enriching experiences. Instead, I am challenging the activity department to take a good look at their list of activities and customize them in highly person-centered ways to make them more meaningful and significant. How do you accomplish that?

Your first task is to get to know your residents—who they were back in their day, and who they are now. Discover what kinds of work they did in the past and inquire about their hobbies, leisure pastimes, and what they prefer for entertainment. Assess the level of stimulation the resident can tolerate. Some will thrive on high-energy activities, while others will be overwhelmed by them. Meaningful activities are those that create opportunities for residents to participate and express their thoughts and feelings, develop self-esteem, build on their strengths and skills, and build a community of others. Creating or discussing music, art, politics, religion, movies, or sports can be interesting and meaningful. Creating a journalism club, designing collages, writing and discussing poetry or short stories, dancing, gardening, and cooking can offer a number of benefits to residents who engage in such activities.

Spontaneous activities are those that anyone in the facility can engage in with residents at any time during the day or night. It is a misguided notion that only the activity staff can or should do fun things with residents. Anyone working in long-term care should be able to take the time to initiate a spontaneous activity with one or several residents—administrators, social workers, nurses, aids, laundry and housekeeping staff, dietary staff—even the maintenance crew! Spontaneous activities occur exactly at the time residents and staff feel like doing something fun, like breaking out a deck of cards and playing poker at midnight when a few residents are still awake and cannot sleep. Other types of spontaneous activities can include board games, snacks, taking a walk outside, reading, and doing arts and crafts. The point of spontaneous activities is that they are unplanned, unstructured, spur-of-the moment, and can occur twenty-four hours a day.

Personalized Structure and Meaningful Activities

I will never forget the first time I met Terry Willingham, ADC, in Cleveland, Ohio. She told me that she comes to work dressed as nine different historical characters including Jacqueline Kennedy Onassis and Annie Oakley. She also has a couple characters that she created, one named Trailer Trash Trixie. She walks around the Alzheimer's unit putting on a show for the residents, some of whom actually believe she is Jackie O! She does the walk, the talk and makes each character come to life. She is the activity director—or, as she calls the position, the quality of life director. I told her that I believe I have met either one of the most creative and energetic activity directors in my career—or she is absolutely insane! Who would go to the great lengths of designing costumes, wearing them at work, and putting on shows for the residents? She would. I now know and appreciate that she is not crazy, but instead is a highly talented and caring professional who loves what she does.

I asked Terry to give me some pointers for a workbook I authored for resident-centered training concerning person-centered activities. She gave me a lot of helpful information that I am now passing on to you. She believes that activities should be structured around the residents' interests, not those of the activity director. The only way to achieve this is to get to know your residents personally. Activities should be uplifting and memorable. Residents do not want to participate in something that bores them. Once you bore them, they may not want to come back. Activities should produce an excitement such that residents look forward to coming back for more fun and cannot wait until the next time the activity is held. When a lot of residents ask for an activity to be repeated—repeat it! A good person-centered activity involves one that stimulates others to get to know each other, interact, and enjoy the social milieu. Residents have the right to complain about anything they want, including activities, recreation, and outings. They also have the right to add their input and personal opinions about the quality of the activity. Getting their input can make an activity more person-centered.

Terry also believes that the director and staff should try to preserve as much continuity as possible, meaning that residents should be able to enjoy things in the facility that they have enjoyed their entire lives. "This," she stresses, "is one of the greatest challenges of person-centered activities." Activity directors and staff must find ways for residents to enjoy their favorite activities from the past at a level and intensity that they can tolerate now. She believes that this one of the reasons people become activity professionals in the first place—for the challenges the job presents and the creativity you get to exercise.

The family can be a great untapped resource for assistance in activities with purpose and meaning. Most of us are used to having family members around us, and much of our time was spent doing things with our family. So, why not get families and friends involved as much as possible in activities, recreation, and outings? It is a good idea to get input from family and friends concerning monthly activities. We also have the obligation to assist families in having meaningful visits with their loved ones in the facility. Inviting them to participate in leisure activities can also bring quality to their lives. Residents don't want to be bored, and families don't want to see their loved one being bored. According to Terry, "It is the duty of every staff member, not just the activities department, to assist the resident in enjoyment of their quality of life, to help them enjoy each day to its fullest, and leave behind old horror stories about nursing homes." This can be achieved through highly personalized and meaningful activities.

New Roles for the Activity Professional

This is a very exciting time to be an activity professional in long-term care. The activity professional is now taking on many new roles thanks to culture change and the person-centered care movement that are evolving in long-term care facilities across the nation. Now, more than ever before, the activity professional can create and deliver meaningful activities that provide purpose and significance in the lives of their residents. Culture change and person-centered care focus on one important aspect of the resident's life—their needs. They represent needs-focused philosophies and ideologies that place the resident in the center of the care process and make their needs top priority. Different people have different needs, so it is important for the activity professional to know what his or her residents need to make them happy and bring them quality of life. Meeting the resident's needs is one important step in increasing his or her quality of life.

Activity professionals have always been necessary in long-term care. Now they can become even more important and significant as they lead the way in culture change, person-centered care, and activities with purpose. Now is the time to move out of your comfort zone and into a new role that will expand your talents and skills while enhancing quality of life. Activity professionals can become "change agents" in long-term care, meaning that they endorse and educate others on culture change, person-centered care, and activities that provide quality of life. They can train others in the facility to provide spontaneous activities twenty-four hours a day, seven days a week.

The activity professional can become a "steering agent," meaning that he or she is continually steering other healthcare professionals to do the right thing for residents, to provide both quality of care and quality of life, and to motivate and encourage staff to have fun and enjoy their residents. Today's activity professional can lead the way to 5-star customer service by leading by example and showing the staff how to provide what residents want—a reason to wake up tomorrow and to enjoy life. Take a chance. Move away from the traditional way of thinking about and delivering activities, and develop a fresh, new approach and perspective. Residents will thank you and love you for it.

Adding It Up

There is a big difference between quality of care and quality of life. Just because we provide nursing, physical therapy, occupational therapy, and medical treatment to residents does not mean that they are living a good quality of life. I believe this is where activity staff are so important to long-term care. They can deliver the fun and exciting aspects of life to residents. They can provide something for residents to look forward to. Without quality of life, I believe that people may simply exist without much meaning or purpose in their lives. This is a very sad thing to me, and I encourage activity professionals to design and deliver activities that make residents feel alive, important, and vital. Offer programs, events, social outings, and parties that mean something to residents. Offer activities that promote purpose and personal growth. Let your creativity flow, and don't hold back. Residents depend on you to bring life and fun to their home. Don't let them down.

POINTS TO PONDER

1. If you were to compare your facility's quality of care and quality of life what are some of the differences between them?

2. What does your facility offer to residents that give them something to look forward to? Why do they want to wake up tomorrow?

3. Does your current activities department offer programs that enhance resident's quality of life? Personal growth? Personhood?

4. How involved are family members in activity programs?

CHAPTER FIVE:
CHANGES IN THE DELIVERY
OF CARE

*Unless someone like you cares a whole awful
lot, Nothing is going to get better. It's not.*

Dr. Seuss

Person-centered care and culture change involve
so much more than changes in dietary services, activities, and redesigning the physical building. Deeply
engrained in these ideas is a fundamental shift in how
we think about and deliver nursing care. Although nursing care is necessary, it should not be the focal point
of the resident's existence in long-term care. Instead,
care is only one aspect of living in a nursing home.
Relationships, choice, preference, and lifestyle should
be the driving forces behind changes in how care is
delivered to residents. The concepts discussed in this
chapter reflect a departure from traditional and institutional care to humane and resident-driven care. They
support the ideas of Brooker's "positive person work"

(pp. 90-95) and Baker's "culture of compassion" (pp. 112-115).

Culture Change Models and the Delivery of Care

Culture change is not an entirely new concept; in fact it has been fashionable to speak of culture change in long-term care for the past twenty-five years. Despite there being several models of culture change, it has yet to fully take off and excel in the United States and other parts of the world. Person-centered care (or resident-centered care) is just one model of change among others, including the hospital-based Planetree Model (Frampton, pp. 3-5), the Eden Alternative (Thomas, pp. 1-3), Wellspring, the Pioneer Network, the Green House Concept (Kane, et al., p. 832), and the House-hold Model (Shields, p. x). All of these models have provided ideas concerning changes throughout the entire facility as well as changes in direct care.

I propose a new and more comprehensive model based on the literature and my observations in nursing homes. It can loosely be called the "Person-Centered Way," just like the title of this book, and involves several key components: flexible care schedules, flexible medication pass, natural waking and retiring, the creation of a new position (the person-centered specialist), self-assignment, self-scheduling, the development of neighborhoods or mini-communities, the differences between treating a resident and caring for a resident, respect for personal daily routines, personal choice and preference, relationships, employee turnover, resident, employee and family satisfaction, and a new role for managers and supervisors—becoming a "steering agent."

Flexible Schedules

Since resident choice and preference are to be respected, flexibility in when care is given, by whom care is delivered, and even where it is provided are all critical aspects in person-centered care. Residents are in more control of their care than is the staff. Even residents diagnosed with dementia can be given more flexibility in their care schedules. They can live a life that is more "natural" and less institutional if we allow for greater accommodation in their daily routines. Some healthcare professionals have found this idea to be rather radical and somewhat risky. Common sense must still prevail, but care doesn't have to be so rigid that it impairs quality of life and takes all the fun out of living.

I sometimes use this analogy when I am training employees to design person-centered care in their facilities: If you were taking care of eight elderly family members in your home, how would you do it? Most likely, you would let them sleep in until they were ready to wake up, have breakfast ready when they wanted to eat, ask them how they wanted to spend their day, provide care in between, and let them retire for the night naturally. This, I believe, is how life should flow in a nursing home with the help of flexible schedules. There are certain routines in long-term care that can be made more flexible, including, but not limited to waking and retiring, morning and afternoon care, med passes, treatments, therapies, meal times, baths and showers, and activities.

Flexible Medication Pass

Medications can be passed by the nurse (or in some states, the medication aid) with the preferences and lifestyle of the resident in mind, upon natural rising, with meals and when the resident goes to bed at night. Physician's orders will have to be re-written as, "Meds to be given at natural rising, meals and retiring," and a flexible med pass policy will need to be written. We will discuss these matters later in the book. The point here is to pass meds when residents want their meds. This has turned a few heads during my training, and several questions have been raised, such as, "What if they never want their meds?" and "What about confused residents?" Flexible med pass doesn't throw common sense out the door and is no reason to discontinue encouraging residents to comply with sound medical advice and remain as healthy as possible. In addition, residents who are non-compliant with medications will continue to be non-compliant with medications (and everything else, for that matter) with or without person-centered care. Flexibility offers residents more choice over when they take their medications based on their natural pattern of living.

Throw Away Your Med Cart

Some facilities around the country have decided to eliminate the use of big, bulky med carts. They instead pass meds the old fashioned way—with a silver tray and Dixie cups full of meds or in wicker baskets. It doesn't matter what the meds are passed in as long as the resident receives the correct meds in a timely manner. Nurses could very well dress up like Little Red Riding Hood and skip gleefully down the hallway with a basket of medications if they want to!

So, what should nurses do with their med carts? Give them to your maintenance crew. I am sure they will finds all kinds of uses for your cart—from a tool box to a place to store nuts, bolts, screws and other small, hard-to-find parts. Give the cart to your activities department. It will be transformed into a pizza shop on wheels. Employees in the activity department are very creative and will find all kinds of fun things for that med cart. I have also seen facilities use stationary cabinets and desks that look like common household furniture, but instead they are built for medication storage, complete with double-lock containers for schedule two medications.

Natural Waking and Retiring

This is a common sense change to creating a more person-centered and household environment—let residents sleep in as long as they want to and allow them to establish their own morning routines. We all have routines that we have lived by for decades, and just because we are old or sick is no reason to be forced into abandoning our routines and learning new, institutional ones. That just doesn't seem fair to me at all. Men and women who have held careers for a lifetime must now conform to the facility's schedule? I don't think so.

Some residents have been early risers their entire lives—so let them get up early. Others have been night owls and prefer to sleep in late and stay up late—so let them. It's a more natural way of life. Second and third shift may be a little busier if residents are up and about, but that's why they are there anyway. This is one reason I believe that food and activities should be available around the clock. They should be able to accompany all tastes and lifestyles, not just one, cookie-cutter, institutional way of life. I have found it almost hysterical and somewhat sad that we wake residents up out of a deep sleep to give them their sleeping pills. I would surely be a non-compliant resident, wouldn't you? The notion of non-compliance itself, especially concerning meds, may become a less severe or a complete nonissue when residents are given the green light to live their lives as naturally as possible.

The Person-Centered Specialist

I owe Dionne Nichol, LNHA, a huge amount of thanks in teaching me years ago about the new position and roles of the universal worker. She and I agree on a lot, but not on the title of this new position. She uses the term "Universal Worker" and I know some other administrators and DONs that use "Universal Employee." I like "Person-Centered Specialist" or PCS for short and for some very good reasons. First and foremost, it uses the word "specialist" and I think that this enhances the nursing assistant's sense of self-worth and esteem. Second, it is exactly what is says—a person-centered specialist in the care of residents. And last, the word "Person" sticks out and reminds us all that we are taking care of people and this is a great calling in life, a privilege, and, to many, a blessing.

What is a person-centered specialist? It is one of the most exciting changes to develop in person-centered care and culture change. It essentially is a new role for direct caregivers or nursing assistants (STNAs) that incorporates cross-training in housekeeping, activities, dietary, and laundry. Some facilities have been doing this for years, but it has finally received more attention. There are still thousands of nursing homes across the country and around the world that have not cross-trained nursing assistants into this new role. Directors of activities, housekeeping, dietary, and laundry take the lead and train nursing assistants how to engage in spontaneous activities, deep clean resident rooms once a week and keep their neighborhood tidy and clean, prepare simple meals in the kitchen or kitchenette, and do a load of clothes when the residents want. The person-centered specialist is a professional who is a certified nursing assistant who cares for eight residents (more or less) and takes care of just about everything in his or her neighborhood. Person-centered specialists can be offered the option of working eight-, ten-, or twelve-hour shifts. Ideally, he or she can also be given the option of self-assignment concerning residents and neighborhoods.

Benefits of the Person-Centered Specialist

Dionne and I have discussed benefits and outcomes of this new position. She has pointed out that the universal worker has become an even more important agent of change in the facility and is absolutely central to the system of care. "In our building, they are seen as the most important employee. Our organizational model is no longer the classic triangle, or bureaucratic top-down structure. It is a flat playing field with no power or authority structures. This is important because a key feature of person-centered care is letting go of control and rigidity over employees (as well as residents)." Another benefit involves the employee's ability to do many jobs and maintain a smaller assignment of residents in their own neighborhood or community. In addition, the employee gets to know residents and builds lasting and trusting relationships with them. Residents benefit because they thrive on familiarity in a loving and genuine environment.

Consistent Assignment

A crucial part of person-centered care involves allowing employees to maintain a consistent assignment on a neighborhood or in a mini-community. Some facilities use employees who "float" a lot throughout the building, but it has been well documented in the literature that this provides little to no benefit for anyone, especially the resident. Most times, floating nurses or aids have little knowledge of the resident and therefore have not had the time to develop trusting, therapeutic relationships with them.

Floating is institutional and not person-centered. Consistent assignments can improve quality of care by understanding the resident's unique personality and needs, by creating a comfort level that enhances compliance and learning the resident's daily routines and behaviors, by encouraging independence, and by monitoring skin integrity and improving ambulation. It can also increase employee morale and retention. Consistent assignments can strengthen relationships, stabilize staff, increase job satisfaction, and improve the quality of care and life for residents. On the other hand, floating or rotating assignments can lead to higher levels of stress and burnout, lower morale, call-offs, and employee turnover. The choice between the two seems simple.

Self-Assignment

Allowing employees to choose which residents they work with and on neighborhoods of their choice are important aspects of person-centered care and culture change. Self-assignment can greatly improve direct care because the employee has the power and decision-making ability to work where they choose and with whom they choose. In other words, they "own" their decisions. This can lead to greater accountability, responsibility, and improved health outcomes for residents and employees. If employees choose where they work, I believe they are more likely to be successful. If they are placed on a unit by a manager or are told where to work, they may not be as satisfied. This can lead to stress, burnout, or turnover. It can also lead to delivery of poor or indifferent care.

Self-Scheduling

When I bring up the idea of employees being allowed to make their own schedules, I really freak out healthcare professionals! Self-scheduling is a concept that has been around for quite some time and has been used in various industries, including health care. It involves abandoning central scheduling or assigning one employee (many times it's a nurse, the director of nursing, or some other manager who acts as the "scheduler"), and creating a system where employees create their own bi-weekly or monthly work schedule. If, for some reason, an employee needs to make a change in their schedule and take a day off, they are completely responsible for calling another employee and getting them to cover.

I have talked to some managers in the field, and they indicate that some companies have tried this and it worked unexpectedly well. Others have told me that they are scared to death to allow their employees to look at, let alone touch or make up their own schedule! It depends on your employees, management, and leadership in the building. I believe that with the right leadership and a culture of trust and responsibility, it can work. And if it does, I also believe that it would have many positive outcomes, including increased accountability and maturity of the workforce, fewer call-offs and no-shows, and a decrease in turnover.

Neighborhoods, Villages, and Mini-Communities

The neighborhood concept is an important part of person-centered care and culture change. It is mentioned in this chapter because it influences direct care and will also be discussed in a later chapter concerning physical changes in the building. Most nursing homes have long, hospital-like hallways and corridors. This gives them an institutional feeling and appearance. One of the goals of person-centered care is to create smaller neighborhoods, villages, or mini-communities within these long hallways. A neighborhood can consist of three or four residents' rooms and is managed by a person-centered specialist. Each neighborhood is unique and has its own personality and character. The point of neighborhoods in this chapter is this—they create smaller environments where residents feel more at home and care is delivered in a more personal and comfortable manner.

Adding It Up

A good way to summarize the points listed in this chapter concerning care changes is discussing the difference between technically "treating" residents and truly "caring" for them. Treating residents (i.e., med pass, wound, and skin care) can become a technical and almost robotic task performed by nurses. Nursing assistants can also treat residents in a distant, mechanical way as if they were objects on an assembly line. I am not accusing anyone of delivering this kind of care, but in some circumstances, it can easily take place as routines, schedules, and tasks dominate the minds of employees and the culture of facilities. The resident is more important than the task.

Person-centered care requires a departure from approaching care in an institutional manner and providing real tender loving care to elderly and frail people who need it. We can move away from treatment and more towards care by creating flexible schedules and med passes, allowing residents to wake up and retire naturally, by allowing staff to self-assign permanently, and by making long hallways smaller through the use of the neighborhood concept. All of these changes can greatly benefit residents and staff and allow for a more natural flow of life to replace institutional living. Choice, preference, and relationships can flourish in this kind of environment. Residents and employees can experience new levels of morale and satisfaction.

For many years in long-term care, I have heard of two buzz words that are encouraged by state and federal regulatory bodies as well as the MDs. Those words are "individualized care." I realize that many good healthcare professionals have tried their best for decades to improve and deliver individualized care. Most professionals do everything they can to provide it. Yet, I know that real, 100%, individualized care has been difficult to achieve because nursing homes have always been total institutions and residents traditionally have been treated as large aggregate groups instead of individuals. What excites me most about person-centered care and the culture change movement is that we can finally begin to deliver the real deal when it comes to individualized care. Person-centered care is a more refined and more highly evolved version of individualized care. We had to start somewhere, but we are finally here. This is something to celebrate and incorporate right away.

POINTS TO PONDER

1. Are there rigid care schedules (i.e. med pass, meal times, therapy times, wake up lists) in your facility and if so, how do they impact resident quality of life?

2. How do you and your staff feel about cross-training STNAs in housekeeping, activities and even in dietary services? Do you like the idea of STNAs becoming "Person-Centered Care Specialists"?

3. Do self-assignment or self-scheduling make you uneasy? Why?

CHAPTER SIX: FROM AN INSTITUTION TO A HOME: ENVIRONMENTAL CHANGES

Man is a child of his environment.

Shinichi Suzuki

"Long-term care facilities are not intended to be mere buildings; they are intended to be meaningful places" (Chapin, p. 3). The physical structure of the facility should be a constant reinforcement of person-centered care and culture change. When employees work in a home-like environment, they may be better able to treat residents as if they were in their own home. If they continue to work in an overly institutionalized facility, both employees and residents are always reminded that they are in a nursing home. This is why either enhancing or redesigning the environment is such an important part of person-centered care and culture change. Environmental psychologists have told us for years about the significant impact our

---

environment has on us. Making changes to the physical structure of the building is no small matter, and there will be some capital investments involved. But when all is said and done, residents will have a place they can call home and employees will have a place where they love to work.

Private and Social Places

If we are going to treat the facility like a home, we must consider how we use physical space in our own homes and think about what those spaces mean to us. In every home, there are private places and social places. The most private rooms in our home are the bedroom and bathroom. We learn at very young ages that these rooms are private, and we need to respect the boundaries of these rooms. Sometimes privacy is violated in long-term care in resident rooms and bathrooms because there are no clear boundaries. Staff may feel that these areas aren't private because they are part of the facility. A complete change in attitude about these private places must take place so that residents feel at ease. If we start redesigning the facility to look more like a home, employees must treat it like a home. There will be clear and visible reminders of privacy—just like the ones we have in our own homes.

The social places we have in our homes are those enjoyed by family and friends and include the kitchen, living room, family room, and dining room. In nursing homes, the kitchen is usually off limits to residents (something that I am personally against), and the common areas such as the dining room are usually large and impersonal. Ideally, these areas should be redesigned to be smaller, so that more intimate social gatherings can take place without getting lost in such a large room. Residents who have hearing or vision impairment can benefit greatly from a smaller, more manageable living area. Larger rooms usually distort auditory and visual stimuli, whereas smaller rooms allow for auditory and visual information to be much closer to the resident.

Shields and Norton provide a number of design principles that can be applied to almost any facility (pp. 33-38). They believe that environmental changes should aim to normalize life by ridding ourselves of institutional thinking, asking residents what they want, making the place more like home, and turning management and staff offices into living space for residents. I strongly believe that we should eliminate nurses' stations and build additional living areas for our residents.

The authors also believe that the resident's home, just like ours, is a sanctuary and should be treated as such. We value our home; it is our most prized possession. It reflects who and what we are and is highly personalized. Any redesign should include intimate and private areas where residents can enjoy their private lives. Home is a place where we greet friends and visitors; we welcome them into our space. Residents, therefore, should have a place where they can greet and host guests, such as a living room, private dining room, library, or den.

The authors feels, as do I, that there should be "child friendly" zones in the facility where children can play video games, have snacks, and interact with other children (under the supervision of an employee) while Mom and Dad are visiting Grandma. Why not give children something to do if they do not wish to visit as long as their parents do?

Shields and Norton recommend a front door that divides large segments of hallways. This can be a simple way to create small neighborhoods. Along with the front door, most houses also have a mailbox, doorbell, porch lights, and a doormat, as well as a front porch and addresses on the siding. You can be as creative as you want to be, but remember to ask the residents what they want their home to be like. The authors also stress the importance of the kitchen in the home and the privacy that our bedrooms offer. Each of these qualities can be incorporated into new design when changing the physical structure of the building.

Any enhancements made to the facility can dramatically change a traditional institution into a supportive and nurturing environment that reminds us of home. Think about the materials that go into building a home: natural wood, indirect lighting, homelike furnishings, and plenty of windows. Building a nursing home that looks like a residential dwelling can produce a number of positive effects on residents such as improved mood and reduced behaviors, increased socialization, and a more relaxed state of mind. An environment like this can reduce stress caused by the environment in a traditional facility that still uses overhead paging, loud call light systems, bright fluorescent lighting, small windows, and brightly tiled floors. We should build places that reduce a resident's blood pressure, not increase it; enhance relaxation, not provoke anxiety; and create a sense of familiarity, not delirium and confusion. One of the overarching goals in remodeling or rebuilding facilities is to provide residents with a home they can call their own—one that is supportive of health, healing, and living. Residents should have access to the kitchen, outdoors, gardens, and other areas that they had access to in their own homes. Residents should have the opportunity to go outside and sit in the sun, rain, sleet, or snow—whichever they prefer, whenever they want to—just like home.

Creating Family Friendly Environments

Resident-directed changes in the environment are only half of the equation. The facility should also make improvements and changes that are considered family and child friendly. I truly believe that more people would visit their loved ones in nursing homes if these places weren't so darned depressing. There are few places where families can visit without interruptions, and there is nowhere for kids to hang out while their parents are visiting their loved one. If we make the environment more visitor friendly, more people, in my opinion, would visit. Family, friends, and the wider community are important to all of us and we thrive on relationships, so why not make the place as nice as we can for these people to visit, have a meal, and get to know us? Our support systems make us strong emotionally and spiri- tuality. They are an important part of our existence, and without them, we wouldn't be the same. Without them, we would become depressed, isolated, withdrawn, and maybe give up on life. I am afraid this is exactly what happens to many elderly residents in nursing homes— they give up on the life they once had and settle for the institutional life they have been handed. I don't find this acceptable anymore, especially when we have such good models for culture change.

When you sit down with your person-centered committee think about integrating family and the com- munity in the design. How do your visitor areas look? Are there enough lounges to accommodate visitors or to hold parties? Is the activities room cluttered? Could it be cleaned up and made into a better space for re- ceiving guests? Have you built small kitchenette areas on each unit or neighborhood? Do residents, visitors, and staff have access to food anytime they want? Is there a place in the facility where you can create a kid zone complete with video games and a snack bar? Are your common areas updated and comfortable? How does the furniture look? Is it all the same design or does it look eclectic and inviting? Overstuffed chairs and couches are popular and make for comfortable seating. Are there enough televisions in common areas if family members want to watch the news, movies, or a sports event?

Using Our Senses to Guide Environmental Change

All environmental changes should start with the requests of residents and family members. After you collect their ideas, get together with your committee and try to use your five senses to guide you in redesign. When I think of most traditional nursing homes, I hate to admit it, but I think of my sense of smell. What does your facility smell like? There will be an offensive odor every now and then, but it should not be permanent. I like the ideas of neighborhoods and kitchenettes because they provide the opportunity to use crock pots, cookie ovens, popcorn machines, bread machines, and other kitchen appliances and devices that create the familiar aromas of home. Each neighborhood can have a baking contest, cookie recipe contest, or best soup of the day contest. The ideas are limitless, and the benefits numerous.

The next sense I use in nursing homes is that of hearing. I once sat at a large round nurses' station with one of the maintenance guys in the middle of the facility (wagon-wheel design). We wanted to count how many bells, whistles, pages, and other unnatural sounds we heard within one hour. We counted over sixty sounds! No wonder employees are stressed out, and residents are agitated. I would be too if I had to hear so many noises every day.

We usually try to reduce the amount of noise in our own homes in order to make the environment more relaxing and enjoyable. I believe that overhead paging should be completely eliminated, and employees should wear silent pagers. Mark Grippi, LNHA, introduced this system in his facility, and it has worked. His employees wear a pager and are completely responsible for it. No one has lost one yet! Instead of overhead pages asking for nurses to "pick up line 1," jazz, and R&B are playing at an appropriate volume throughout the facility. What a difference this has made. Carpet can be used wisely to reduce noise throughout the facility. Most facilities are moving away from carpeted hallways because of staining and accidents as well as difficulty in maneuvering wheelchairs. Utility rooms should be far removed from living areas to further reduce environmental noise. The goal here is not to make the place as silent as a mausoleum, but to recreate the sounds of home—not an institution.

Sight is the next sense I think of when visiting nursing homes, particularly because many do not use fluorescent lighting or natural lighting very well. There is a trend in newer home design to use indirect lighting so that the glare isn't shining in your face and to build larger windows to let the natural sunlight and moonlight into the facility. Florescent lighting is institutional and has been shown to cause stress, anxiety, headaches, and muscle strain. Most people just don't like to be under florescent lighting all day and all night—unless they're in Las Vegas! Draperies and blinds should be used to allow residents control over their environment. Some people like a lot of sunlight shining in through the window, and some do not. Any alteration should have the resident's wishes in mind.

Color schemes play an important role in the environment and can influence residents' mood and emotions. Facilities that are redesigning to be more person-centered are doing away with institutional colors and wallpapers and are using more vibrant paints. Color can be used to create pathways throughout the facility, especially for residents who have dementia. Color can be used to support the function of space (i.e., paint smaller rooms neutral colors, and don't be afraid to go bold in larger areas). Use colors that reduce stress, uplift mood, and make people feel at home. You can also use colors to create something that is interesting, aesthetically pleasing, or stimulating.

Taste is another sense that should be maximized as much as possible by the environment. The kitchen is obviously important when it comes to great food, but so is almost any employee or family member in the facility. Anyone can bring in a crock pot and make a soup of the day, bake cookies or brownies, pop popcorn, or make something that creates aromas of home. Nothing says "home" like a fresh loaf of bread or chocolate chip cookies baking in the oven.

The last sense is touch, and this is equally as important as all of the other senses. When redesigning the facility, try to pick out upholsteries with textile patterns. They may be more comfortable and soothing for residents with dementia. If you do choose wallpaper, there are lots of great textured papers and wall coverings on the market that can give any room an enhanced appearance. Try to purchase as many natural wood products as you can, including chairs, tables, desks, armoires, and night stands. Wood has a natural and soothing feel that most people like. Also try to purchase natural wood cabinets. Non-skid floor coverings are becoming popular and offer another type of texture to a resident's room.

There are many ways to enhance the environment or redesign altogether using the resident's preferences and your five senses as a guide. Try to break away from the traditional, institutional nursing home mindset concerning design. Do something completely different and homelike. Make sure it is comfortable and user friendly. You don't want to create a museum of beautiful artifacts that no one can touch. As Shields and Norton remind us "*Home* means this is where you live, not pretend this is your home" (p. 166).

The Neighborhood Concept

A popular feature of person-centered care and culture change involves deinstitutionalizing long, hospital-like hallways, and dividing them into smaller neighborhoods, villages or mini-communities. The word "neighborhood" is most often used, so I will focus on this concept. An essential goal of the neighborhood is to bring residents and the person-centered specialist closer together to share a smaller, more manageable space. Another goal is to allow residents to direct their lives as they wish—to maintain their own routines and daily activities. Responsibilities and chores can be mutually shared by residents and caregivers, who are responsive, resident-oriented employees. There is no real need for centralized management, because each neighborhood will be taken care of by the person-centered specialist and residents. The individuals living and working in each neighborhood can customize and decorate the environment they way they choose and create a name for their own neighborhood. Contests can be held to determine who has the cleanest neighborhood or the best decorated for the holidays.

This concept not only adds a fun twist to long-term living, it can produce a number of psychological, social, spiritual, and physical benefits. Residents may experience more peaceful living and less stress than that produced by larger, more stimulating environments. Negative behavioral responses such as combativeness, aggressiveness, and non-compliance may diminish as well as the need for psychotropic medications. Feelings of loneliness, helplessness, and hopelessness may decrease by living in a family-oriented neighborhood. Families may feel more comfortable participating in the life of the neighborhood and join in for meals and activities or simply enjoy visiting more often. Employees can benefit from being close to the residents they choose to care for in the neighborhood they select. They lead themselves with no micro-management. Residents, families, and caregivers all share a living space that is comfortable and peaceful.

They organize their day the way they want to and live spontaneously and naturally. They make up their own minds concerning how they will spend their days—going on outings, gardening, listening to music or watching movies, making a meal together, baking cookies, playing cards, reading scripture, or doing nothing at all. It's completely up to them, and the neighborhood model encourages this kind of living.

Turning Shower Rooms into Spas

I mentioned to a group of nursing home professionals that some facilities were redecorating their shower rooms to resemble a spa, and within a few days, they had transformed their shower room into a beautiful spa for their residents. Some shower rooms look like something from one of those frightening *Saw* movies—and we wonder why residents put up a fight when it's time to take a shower. I wouldn't want to spend any time in those rooms, let alone confused and naked.

Here is what the one facility did. They started by removing everything from the shower room and applying a fresh coat of lavender paint. They purchased cloth shower curtains, art work, candles, aromatherapy products, aftershave products, large towels and an electric towel warmer, a Queen Anne chair and wine table, bath and shower soaps, body washes and shampoos, and a shower-safe CD player—all for around $400. All it took was an idea, creativity, and a small amount of money, and they had the spa up and running in no time.

Adding It Up

The aim of this chapter is not to outline each and every architectural change that can be made in nursing homes. Instead, it is meant to provide some ideas concerning better use of the environment and to spark your imagination for making personalized changes in your building that will provide a better standard of living for residents. Whether you choose to transform your shower rooms into spas, build pseudo-house entries at the beginning of each unit, use siding and awnings on the inside of the hallways, or use indirect sconce lighting is up to your residents, families, and you. Dionne Nichol, LNHA, reminds us, "It is important to focus on the environment of the home and stay away from the institutional feel." Change the institution into a home and make it as comfortable as possible for your residents. Allow residents to decorate their rooms as they want. If they want to paint their room a different color, go out and buy a gallon of paint and do it. Meet with your residents and families monthly at resident council or a special person-centered care committee and ask them what they would like to see in terms of changes in the physical plant. I know that everyone's wishes cannot all be honored, but it's nice to open up lines of communication and let people's voices be heard.

POINTS TO PONDER

1. Examine the physical layout of your facility. Are there areas throughout the building that could be transformed into resident living or social space?

2. How much privacy do your residents have in the facility?

3. Are there areas in the building that can be transformed into child-friendly zones?

4. Do your five senses bring you satisfaction or displeasure in your facility? Which areas need to be changed or greatly improved?

5. If you had to move into your facility right now, would you be happy? Would you look forward to activities? Would the quality and service of food be satisfying? Would you like taking baths or showers in your facility's shower room?

CHAPTER SEVEN:
CREATING A NEW CULTURE OF
DEMENTIA CARE

Lord, keep my memory green.

Charles Dickens

"Can individuals diagnosed with dementia and Alzheimer's disease benefit from person-centered care?" This is a question I hear over and over again from healthcare professionals who doubt that this model can be applied to elderly demented residents. "With all of the freedoms of choice and preferences, isn't this dangerous for the confused or mentally ill person?" I usually respond by referring to the work of Dr. Thomas Kitwood who first applied the person-centered care model in dementia and Alzheimer's care units in England. It wasn't until several years later that other authors started using the term to refer to a model of culture change in hospitals and nursing homes. Person-centered care was originally meant to be a prototype of care for individuals who are demented.

Whether residents have dementia or not, they are still the center of the care process, and their needs, desires, and preferences come first. Everything else that caregivers are concerned about, such as their tasks, procedures, routines, or schedules, are all secondary. The relationship between residents and their caregivers is critical so that trust and familiarity can be developed. The better the relationship, the more knowledge the caregiver will have about those for whom they care. Everything that we have examined in this book can be applied to the care of residents diagnosed with dementia. Flexibility in care schedules and meal times are also very important on the dementia unit and can lead to a decrease in stress and negative behaviors. Consistent staff should work in special units—especially in dementia and Alzheimer's units. The unit can be broken down into a few neighborhoods, and spontaneous activities can take place around the clock.

In many of my training sessions, I have argued that behavior management, particularly for residents on a dementia unit, should be person-centered. We must try to return decision making to our residents, even if they are mildly or moderately confused. Similarly, we must open up lines of supportive and therapeutic communication. When these two ingredients are added to a person-centered dementia unit, quality of care and life can be greatly enhanced. Before we can begin to move in a more person-centered direction, we need to understand what we are moving away from and moving towards.

Traditionally, demented residents have been viewed as adults who are losing their memories, abilities, and possibly their personhood. There is no hope for them, there is no cure, and medications are hit-and-miss. These types of residents should be placed on a special unit where they can be more easily supervised by employees. The environment should be modified in such a way that accidents and risks are reduced as much as possible. Negative behaviors are caused by the disease itself, and residents are labeled as "feeds," "wanderers," "hitters," and "escapees." We house them in special units and care for their physical needs until they die.

In contrast, person-centered care teaches us to view the whole person, not just their disease. Dementia is only a small part of the make-up of the entire person. Person-centered care views the person as alive and responsive, able to participate in meaningful activities, and able to share of themselves in ways that provide purpose in life. The unit should be designed in ways that enhance the individual's experience, not diminish it by being overly protective and risk free.

What Are Behaviors?

Traditionally, behaviors may be regarded as negative reactions from residents such as verbal or physical aggression, agitation, wandering, rummaging, refusing personal care, or repeated crying out. When residents display such behaviors, employees rely on interventions from the care plan (which nobody seems to know) such as "redirection" or "distraction," and when these don't work, they may request sedating medications from the attending physician. In a person-centered setting, behaviors are viewed in a completely different way. I believe that behaviors originate from five sources: 1) they are attempts to communicate; 2) they are expressions of unmet needs and feelings; 3) they are reactions to internal stimuli such as pain or hunger; 4) they are reactions to external stimuli including the environment, employees, and other residents; and 5) they originate from biochemical imbalances and/or destruction of acetylcholine and other neurotransmitters in the brain. We sometimes refer to these in traditional care as "triggers" of negative or difficult behaviors.

Brooker (2007) believes that most behaviors can be explained as struggles of the individual to communicate. She states, "In person-centered care, we try to see meaning in all behavior and use this as a starting point for trying to help those in distress" (p. 79). We must attempt to understand what the resident is trying to tell us and not become frustrated ourselves. This can be achieved once we get to know the resident well and learn to interpret their patterns of behavior. This is no easy task and it does involve challenges, but that is why we are in long-term care, is it not? There is a difference between traditional behavior "management" and behavior appreciation or empathizing. I am not quite sure we can "manage" the behaviors of a resident diagnosed with dementia unless we use physical or chemical restraints, and this is not considered person-centered dementia care.

If primary needs and feelings are not recognized or met, the resident may become agitated and display "behaviors." In this instance, the behavior is a cry for attention as well as a message that the resident's needs and feelings are being ignored or unrecognized. The needs that Kitwood outlined, including comfort, attachment, inclusion, occupation, and identity, are important to remember in this discussion (Kitwood, pp. 80-84). These needs and many others can be discovered by getting to know the resident as much as possible and learning his or her unique personality and daily routines.

Residents may also react in upsetting ways if they become overwhelmed by internal or external stimuli. Things like pain or discomfort, the need for control and independence, hunger, or thirst may drive the resident to become agitated and aggressive. Noise, lighting, crowds, or the need to be social may also induce negative reactions. I believe that one of the most common reasons for behaviors is the very nature of most facilities: they are too regimented and over medicalized. In other words, they are institutions. Sometimes we expect residents who are cognitively impaired to conform to the routines of the facility. Instead, we should be conforming to their personal routines. There is an inherent inability to communicate needs here, but I believe the important point is that caregivers do everything they can to maintain a therapeutic environment, spend a good amount of time with their residents, and manage their own behaviors. I truly believe that many behaviors can be diminished or eliminated completely when residents live comfortably in an environment that reminds them of their home with a staff that is well trained and prepared to deliver the best care possible for their residents.

Lastly, behaviors may be a result of biochemical changes taking place in the diseased brain, and unfortunately, I don't believe there is any silver bullet intervention for this. It is well documented that a number of changes take place in the brain due to the Alzheimer's disease process, including a decrease in acetylcholine and interruptions in other neurotransmitters like serotonin and norpinephrine. Despite this, I believe that providing a person-centered environment will do much to reduce behaviors from any origin or source. Creating a natural pace to life, removing institutional barriers, training a caring staff, and getting to know residents are the basics to effectively and humanely handling behaviors.

Common Behaviors

When I train healthcare professionals on dealing with difficult behaviors, I start with the question: "What are the most common behaviors you see on Alzheimer's units?" The responses usually include sundowning, combativeness, screaming, and escaping. Once, I asked a group of nurses and nursing assistants who worked on special care units in Columbus, Ohio, to identify the most difficult behaviors they observe daily. They answered in a way that I will never forget and that I found brilliant. They replied: "The most common behavior problem we have around here is boredom!"

Once I heard their response, a light bulb went off in my mind. It's true—there isn't much to do on a special care unit. The days must be long and dull, and the nights, equally long and boring. When people are bored, they may get themselves into trouble. They may start doing things they wouldn't normally do. Boredom is one of the most common reasons why residents in long-term care develop behaviors. Besides boredom, helplessness, hopelessness, loneliness, depression, and anxiety are probably the most common behaviors in nursing homes. William Thomas (of the Eden Alternative) wrote in 1996 of the "nursing home plagues" including loneliness, helplessness, and boredom (pp. 23-25). These problems are nothing new, but there is great hope in person-centered living as a way to reduce or eliminate these problems.

Changing Ourselves to Improve Dementia Care

Since a reasonable amount of negative resident reactions stem from the caregiver's approach, language, and attitude, I feel this is an important topic to discuss when implementing person-centered dementia care in your building. Engaging in behavior management must start with managing ourselves. What does this mean? It means that we change how we think about long-term care and working with demented residents. How we communicate and behave towards residents can greatly affect them. The attitudes of caregivers may influence the delivery of care and how the resident feels during interaction. Residents who are demented are demented—not stupid! They can pick up on negative attitudes and feelings emanating from the caregiver. If the caregiver is in a rush, residents can feel it and become overwhelmed or emotionally upset. When caregivers are angry, they can create an angry response from residents. The point is—manage your own emotions, attitudes, and feelings when you are working with residents.

Try to put yourself in the shoes of your residents. Instead of viewing their agitation as a negative behavior, see it as a way for them to express energy, assertiveness, and determination. When you want something, regardless of your mood, you try to get it—and so do demented residents. Instead of describing residents as "rummaging" around in other resident rooms, see them as trying to find something familiar and comforting.

I have always disliked the word "wandering." It reminds me of what zombies do in horror films—brainless, soulless zombies wandering about looking for their next victim. Rather than seeing residents as wanderers, see them as explorers and comfort seekers. They are simply exploring the building and looking for something to make them happy and calm.

Other words that I don't like are "escaping" or "eloping." These words literally mean to flee or run away from someone or something. I must say that I have seen a few nursing homes that I would run away from myself. Instead of seeing residents as escapees, try viewing them as on a mission or as focused and determined to get away from an environment that causes them distress.

Non-compliance or refusing personal care can be viewed differently as being self-sufficient, protective of one's self, or maintaining modesty. Crying out repeatedly can be viewed as an exercise in assertiveness and seeking solutions to unmet needs and feelings. And finally, negative behavioral reactions can be viewed as natural responses to the environment or other stimuli. I believe if we change our language, we change our thoughts and ideas, and ultimately we change the way we act and behave. In this sense, true culture change relies on personal changes within us.

When we change our focus from the task, the schedule, and the job at hand and shift the attention to the resident, we can change our attitudes about them. Shifting the focus can take pressure off of caregivers, and they may feel less pressured to get the "job" done and instead care for the resident's needs. When there is more time to spend with residents, caregivers can learn their life stories and incorporate their lifestyles into everyday care. Relationships can be formed and caregivers can encourage residents to participate in as much care as they cognitively and physically can handle. There will be bonds of trust—just like in a family. Spending more time with residents also sends the message to families that we value their loved one and that they are not just another body to clean, clothe, and feed. Have fun with your residents and allow them to live in the moment. People with dementia should be encouraged to grow everyday in some way—either physically, emotionally, socially, psychologically, or spiritually. Let your new focus of person-centered dementia care be "growth."

Kitwood indicates that the new agenda for dementia care is to improve the quality of interactions between caregivers and residents through what he calls "positive person work" (p. 87). The qualities he discusses reflect true culture change and a person-centered approach to working with demented residents. They also suggest a change in caregiver attitude, behavior, language, and approaches. Kitwood's qualities of positive person work are recognition, negotiation, collaboration, play, timalation, celebration, relaxation, validation, holding, facilitation, creation, and giving. These are a complete shift from managing and controlling difficult behaviors through plan of care interventions that may or may not work and of which caregivers may or may not be aware. Traditionally, employees attempt to manage or control resident behavior through the use of psychotropic medications and restraints. The qualities of positive person work represent a kinder, more humane approach to care and the quality of life on special care units.

Setting the Mood on the Dementia Unit

Professional caregivers are influential in terms of the energy they bring to an environment. If an employee comes to work after a fight with a loved one at home, they may bring that negative energy to the unit, and soon other employees as well as residents feel that something is wrong. One of the most important responsibilities of a professional caregiver is to set the mood or the tone of the environment. How is this accomplished? Your mood and emotional state should be positive and healthy. Your body language and facial expressions tell the world what you are feeling inside, so remember to be pleasant. Your approach with residents should be calm and loving. Use their name and speak gently in a volume and tone they can hear and understand. Use short sentences and keep your message simple. Incorporate life histories into daily routines to make activities and life as meaningful and purposeful as possible.

Treat your residents like adults, because that is what they are—they are not children. It drives me crazy when I see healthcare professionals treating cognitively impaired elders like children or babies. This is called infantilization and is completely inappropriate and unacceptable.

Make sure that you are organized in your own care routines and have the materials you need to provide programs, activities, or meals. Don't be afraid to use touch when appropriate and hug your residents. Celebrate each and every day and always end your time with them with a big, cheerful "Thank you!"

Adding It Up

The best place to start in delivering person-centered dementia care is to learn everything you can about each resident's background. Social services, admission directors, or the activity director usually complete some kind of personal information or life history form on each newly admitted resident, so use that information. I would recommend creating your own biographical form and having someone on the unit interview the resident and family to gather information. Then share it with all caregivers on that unit. Discover who these people were before Alzheimer's or dementia started to develop. Were they judges, teachers, physicians, business owners, or nurses? There are many years of experience and intelligence in these people. Simply because they have dementia, we should not disregard everything that they once were. Learn where they are in their cognitive abilities. This will help in appreciating what kinds of activities that can and cannot be tolerated. Don't expect them to meet you where you are—you must meet them where they are cognitively and emotionally. Instead of trying to use reality orientation, use validation. Does it really matter if they know who the current president is or what year it might be? Validation is much more effective in handling emotional challenges and confusion because it focuses on the resident's emotions not their clarity of thought.

Along with the personal history sheet that you can create, I recommend designing a personal timeline for each resident on the unit. This documents when and where they were born, the names of their family members including spouses and siblings, where they went to school, their profession or occupation, information on their marriage including when and where they were married, information on their children, hobbies and leisure activities, favorite pets and any other personal information that can give caregivers all they need to get to know about their residents on a deeper, more intimate level. Ask family members and friends to bring in any artifacts they may have that the resident would recognize and appreciate. You can also ask family members to video tape or record a message to their loved one and then play it from time to time when the resident is feeling lonely or asks for it. Invite family members to assist in decorating and personalizing their loved one's room and bring in furniture or other items that would give them pleasure. Always remember: person-centered care and culture change is about what the resident wants, not what we want for them.

POINTS TO PONDER

1. Examine more closely the roots of your resident's negative behaviors. Are they attempts to communicate something to the staff? Are they attempting to express their unmet needs? What are their unmet needs and what can you do about them?

2. How might the facility's environment produce or promote negative behaviors?

3. Do your employees set a negative tone on units (i.e. Alzheimer's, dementia or gero-psych) where residents may be especially vulnerable to reacting negatively or catastrophically?

CHAPTER EIGHT: INTRODUCING "FAMILY-CENTERED CARE"

Families are like fudge—mostly sweet with a few nuts.

Author Unknown

I am sure that you have heard of the old saying, "You just don't marry the person, you marry their entire family." For better or for worse, this holds true in long-term care. When you agree to take care of a new resident, you also take care of their family. Family-centered care can be just as important as person-centered care; as matter of fact, I believe they are one in the same. Adopting this kind of attitude will enhance customer service and support to families. Exceptional customer service is one of the foundations of a person- and family-centered culture. We must be sensitive to each family's unique needs and feelings, learn as much as we can about them, and learn to appreciate their values. Everyone is a winner when we deliver great customer service—residents, families, and employees are more satisfied and the building is full.

What Do Families Want?

Handing over elderly parents and other loved ones to our care in nursing homes is not an easy thing, and there is no one who looks forward to the day this happens. Many families experience guilt, depression, anxiety, poor adjustment, and various forms of stress. This is by far one of the most difficult things many of us will have to do. Because it is so stressful, healthcare professionals should go out of their way to make families feel that they have done the right thing. Families want someone they can trust, talk to, and turn to when they have questions or difficulties concerning their loved one. They want and deserve clear and genuine communication with the administrator, social worker, nursing staff, and others. Family members may want to develop relationships with nursing assistants who take direct care of their loved one. I always encourage nursing assistants to form trusting and therapeutic relationships with families.

Families need reassurance that they have chosen the right place for Mom or Dad, so staff should be responsive to their needs. Responding to families is a good indicator that employees are also responding to the needs of residents. Families are always observing and judging the facility and staff, so be friendly and pay attention to their needs. Edgman-Levitan found that healthcare professionals may not comprehend how negative perceptions affect patients and their families. "The dissonance between the perspective of families and that of the hospital staff can be enormous" (p. 45). Baker stresses that families may not feel welcomed because of negative staff attitudes (p. 155). Mistrust and poor communication between families and employees can cause a lot of problems. It may be difficult to re-establish relationships, so get them right from the start.

Family members also want help in dealing with special needs and concerns of their loved one. For instance, making decisions about the use of psychotropic medications can be traumatic to some family members, and they may need to speak to the director of nursing, attending physician, or a psychiatrist. Whatever the need is, we should be responsive. Families also want to be educated on things like medications, diseases, and disorders. We can all assist in educating them or finding appropriate resources that can benefit their loved ones as well as themselves.

Some families may want to attend care conferences and other meetings, and some families may have no interest at all. Regardless, it is up to us to make these meetings as family friendly as we can. Try to schedule them around the time constraints of the family, offer refreshments, invite their loved one, and make the meeting as efficient as possible. Family members also want competent employees who care about residents. They want their loved one to feel comfortable and at home. They want their loved one to feel safe and welcomed. They want to make sure we have enough staff on the floors and that we are not working "short." Families do not want to see a new caregiver every day—a result of turnover or floating. They would like to see managers treating employees with dignity and respect and see caregivers treating residents the same way. If you haven't asked families in your facility what they want recently, you may be dropping the ball concerning family-centered care.

I train healthcare professionals on how to work with difficult family members, and one way to be successful is to get them involved in your person-centered care committee at the beginning of the program. Families want to have a voice in how their loved one is cared for and where they live in the facility. They may have issues (complaints) about a number of things including lost laundry, eyeglasses, dentures, and hearing aids. They may complain about the food or particular employees. Involving families in the de-institutionalization of your facility will most likely lead to a significant decrease in problems or complaints. I have spoken to a number of administrators, directors of nursing, and others who have implemented person-centered care and they have all indicated the same thing—family complaints have diminished to almost nothing. Especially concerning food, they have no complaints. This is a rather significant change in nursing home culture.

Getting Families Involved

To serve families even better, I believe that we should invite them to eat breakfast, lunch, or dinner with residents at no cost. What a better way to say, "You are always invited to our home"? This will be particularly nice if you implement family- or home-style dining. Encourage them to become part of the community and culture of the facility. Visiting hours should not be restricted to certain times, since family members work different shifts and a strict visitation policy may create barriers and undue stress. Family members are family members—they are not visitors. Make sure that you have a designated space in the building for families, not just to visit, but somewhere they can go to unwind and relax before or after their visit. If they wish to bring their pets into the facility for a visit, invite them to do so, especially if the resident will benefit. Sometimes family members will want to stay for long periods of time to provide care for their loved one themselves. Some managers may see this as a risk management issue, but I believe it can be handled lightly and appropriately.

We can encourage families to become more involved if they feel that they are part of the team. It is okay to develop friendships with family members. Friends welcome friends into their home. Friends also know each others' names, so always try to use family members' names when addressing them. Accept their opinions and recommendations with an open mind and let them know that the staff will do everything it can to see their wishes materialize, especially if they are good ideas. Keep them informed of any changes taking place in the building—such as room changes or construction projects. To develop a family-centered culture, you must get to know who they are and what their personalities are like. They want us to have personal information, for the most part. They want us to know everything about their loved one that will help in delivering a high quality of care and creating a wonderful quality of life. If you want more family involvement in your facility, ask for it. You may be surprised at the results.

Another way to stimulate family involvement is to establish family councils, family-centered groups and other family-oriented meetings in your facility on a routine basis. I was amazed when I spoke to an activity director who told me she had seventy-five family members as volunteers. She always had good family involvement in the facility, but after implementing person-centered care, the numbers increased dramatically. She said, "Families are excited about person-centered care and invite it with opened arms." They want to become a part of the program and help make changes in the facility to meet the needs and desires of their loved ones. They see person-centered care as a way they, too, can make a difference. It is such a refreshing sight to see. In one facility, family members donate dozens of bottles of wine, whiskey, gin, and vodka for their bar. Once while visiting the facility, I saw several bottles of alcohol on the activity director's desk and thought to myself, "Does she have a drinking problem—and at work to boot!?" She didn't have a drinking problem—the bottles were all donated by families who wanted the residents to have access to adult beverages when they wanted.

Influencing How Employees View Families

It has been my experience that some employees in long-term care (and probably in other care facilities such as hospitals and assisted living) see families as the enemy, intruders, or a pain in the neck. They surely do not view them as a vital part of the care team or as partners. I think we are dropping the ball if this is how employees regard families. Some employees may see families as people who complain about things even when there is nothing to complain about or as just picky and unappreciative and nothing will make them happy. A note of reality is necessary here before I continue—I know there are some difficult families out there and in some facilities, there exists real tension between the care staff and some family members. After all, I train healthcare professionals how to deal effectively with them. But, I also believe that a lot of difficulties can be minimized through person-centered care and a little bit of common sense.

Baker states that "transformational homes are places where families feel welcome and happy to visit" (p. 158). It seems to me that it is much easier to attract more bees with honey than with vinegar. Plus, being nice doesn't cost anything. You may be surprised to see negative or high-maintenance families turn around when they are invited to assist you in making culture changes in the facility.

Some families may see the benefits right up front, and others may be nervous or frightened by the process. Believe it or not, both reactions are helpful and healthy for you to use in transforming the facility. Person-centered care may mean care with more dignity to some families and to others it may mean that their diabetic father will be allowed to eat whatever he wants, whenever he wants, and this is going to kill him. Being family-centered means you address every concern and provide education concerning the best outcomes for the residents. Family friendly homes take a relationship-based approach to assisting and educating families and creating a level of comfort and peace of mind. Frampton, et al., remind us to "never separate family members from the patient—unless the patient requests it. Healing and recovery are enhanced by the love and support offered by a patient's community of family and friends. If we learn to incorporate that support, we will no longer be at odds with those who love and know the patient best" (p. 68).

Outcomes of a Family-Centered Culture

There isn't enough space in this chapter for me to document all of the possible positive outcomes when person-centered care is implemented in the facility and family-centered care is adopted by employees. Among the many that I have observed or read about in the literature, increased resident, family, and employee satisfaction are among some of the most common outcomes. When satisfaction is enhanced among residents, decreased behaviors, a reduction in psychotropic drugs, and improved quality of life can all become reality. You may also observe better appetites when residents eat with their families and better sleep habits after gratifying visits. When family satisfaction is improved, we may gain more information about loved ones, which will allow us to provide better care for them. Families may complain less or not at all, and may not threaten the facility with lawsuits. Complaints brought to the ombudsman will probably decrease as well. As employee satisfaction increases, care and quality of life improve, staff can lower their defenses and enjoy family interaction, and they can provide the kind of care they have always wanted to provide—resident- and family-centered care.

Adding It Up

I have always believed that when a new resident is admitted to the facility, we not only care for them, but for their entire family as well. This can be a rewarding experience, and sometimes a stressful one. A family is like a box of chocolates, to borrow a line from *Forrest Gump*, because we never know what we are going to get. Regardless, we have an ethical obligation and duty to provide the best care and the highest quality of living possible to our residents and to reach out to their families and provide them with whatever they may need. If you aren't sure what the family members want or need—ask them. Most want information and support. Reaching out to families and forming genuine relationships with them can be beneficial for the resident, employee, and census.

POINTS TO PONDER

1. What letter grade (i.e. A, B, C, D, or F) would you give your staff and building in terms of family-friendliness? How would you grade each department throughout the facility?

2. How well do you know families in your facility? Are there a few that you don't know well? What can you and your staff do about it?

3. How would you grade the involvement of your families in the facility? If it is poor, why?

4. Do your coworkers view family members as visitors or partners?

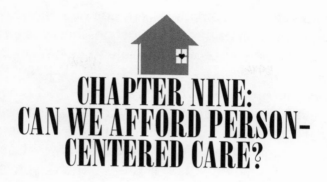

CHAPTER NINE: CAN WE AFFORD PERSON-CENTERED CARE?

> *If money is your hope for independence, you will never have it. The only real security that a man will have in this world is a reserve of knowledge, experience, and ability.*
>
> **Henry Ford**

One of the most disconcerting things I hear from some healthcare professionals is, "Person-centered care will cost our facility too much money." I usually respond by saying, "You cannot afford *not* to implement person-centered care in your facility. Not only will you fail to improve quality of life for your residents, you will also run the risk of being twenty years behind everyone one else in long-term care." Finances are always an issue to be discussed and costs are important—but not to the point where they make the facility antiquated. As I travel from state to state, I see many nursing homes that were built in the 1970s and 1980s that are ready for an overhaul. If companies are going to spend money on renovation or new construction, then it is time to upgrade to person-centered care and cultural restoration.

Improving quality of life for residents and modernizing the building are not the only benefits of investing in person-centered care. Although there are some capital investments that initially will be somewhat costly, there are many operational areas where you save money. Labor costs are the most expensive item on the budget, and employee turnover is rather high in many traditional nursing homes. Person-centered care can save money by reducing turnover, absenteeism, and use of temporary agencies in your facility. Food costs are usually the second most expensive area on the budget, and the ugly truth about food in long-term care is that up to 50% of it is thrown out every day. No one benefits from wasted food, and person-centered care can minimize food waste and the need for expensive dietary supplements and specialized diets. As quality of care improves through the person-centered model, clinical expenses can also be reduced.

Baker reminds us that "high-quality care is actually *less* expensive to deliver than low-quality care" (p. 189). Better care can lead to a reduction in falls and accidents, pressure sores, UTIs, and the need for expensive psychotropic drugs and incontinence products. Liability claims can be trimmed down and results of annual state surveys can be improved. Another area that can benefit greatly is the census. Many facilities that have moved to a person-centered model have waiting lists and very few census-related problems. This model is not only good for residents, families, and employees, it's good for business. All of these benefits do not come without some level of risk, but you will see that the benefits far outweigh the risks after reading this chapter.

Make a promise to yourself before continuing. Promise that you will approach this chapter with an open mind and abandon what Shields and Norton refer to as "scarcity thinking" (pp. 154-155). They believe, "The traditional nursing home model has created a mindset of scarcity thinking. We too often assume 'we can't' as a matter of course. Consequently, we have developed a culture of 'make do with what we've got.'" They also remind us that some operators are penny wise and pound foolish when it comes to expenses and potential. If you, your staff, and the company culture is one of scarcity thinking, promise to examine how you think about money and the potential income your facility can have if you make some key changes. Think about making more money, increasing census, and improving quality of work for employees and quality of life for residents. Think about this: "If you truly can't afford the capital, in most cases it means your organization has a limited lifespan" (Shields and Norton, p. 156).

Labor Expenses and Potential Savings

Since labor costs are the most expensive operating cost in the budget, it makes sense to begin looking at the enormous amount of money that is wasted due to turnover, absenteeism, and using agencies and the potential for savings through increased employee retention. Annual turnover rates among nursing assistants is 70–100%, and turnover among nurses, including DONs, runs around 50% (Baker, pp. 62-63). Estimates run as high as $2.5 billion in wasted money due to turnover.

What costs are involved in hiring employees and replacing them? We have take into account many costs involving advertising, interviewing, screening, physicals, TB tests, the hepatitis B vaccination, drug screens, hiring bonuses or employee referral bonuses, criminal background checks, overtime and double-time of employees covering, and orientation and training. The average cost to replace one nursing assistant ranges between $2,500 and almost $4,000 depending upon geographical location. If the industry average for turnover starts at around 70%, multiply 70 by $3,000, and what we end up with is an annual loss of $210,000 for every 70 nursing assistants alone in an average facility. This is a huge amount of wasted money and talent, and it doesn't have to be this way. Other employees including social workers, occupational and physical therapists, and activities professionals are very costly and leave their place of employment for many reasons, but it all boils down to employee satisfaction.

Adequate staffing is the key to running a stable operation. Reducing staff turnover and absenteeism can lead to a cost benefit for the facility. When you are operating with a stable staff, quality of care increases, customer satisfaction increases, and, ultimately, census increases. Operating with a stable staff can also reduce dependency and costs of temporary agency staff. Some facilities report spending $2–4 million annually on agency staff, so clearly, stabilizing staff in your facility can save a huge amount of money.

When it comes to saving money or breaking even on labor costs, Dionne Nicole, LNHA, states, "There was no change in finances. All changes were accomplished within the guidelines of our budget. Changing to the universal worker had no change on the direct care PPDs. Although you have to pay the housekeeper and activity assistants more money as they become universal workers, you are at the same time cutting down your PPDs in activities and housekeeping, which equals out the whole process." There are other benefits that evolve when we create a stable work force, reduce turnover and absenteeism, cross-train caring and intelligent employees, and minimize or eliminate agency staff. Residents, families, and employees are satisfied, we have better annual state surveys, and we have a full house with a waiting list.

Dietary Costs and Savings

Food costs are the next big expense on the facility budget. It is an accepted fact that many healthcare facilities throw out a lot of food—some up to 50%. What a waste! Why do we throw away so much food in long-term care? Because no one wants to eat it! Typically, the dietary manager orders food from vendors that he or she thinks the residents will like. Meanwhile, residents have no say in what they are eating on a daily basis. Residents will not eat food that isn't well prepared and doesn't look appetizing. All of this translates into a terrible waste of food, money, and time.

Person-centered dining can be provided within your current budget, can save money, and will lead to numerous quality outcomes. When residents are given the opportunity to eat what they want, they improve their dietary habits and require fewer costly dietary supplements or specialized and prescribed diets. Better diets may mean a need for fewer expensive psychoactive medications including anti-depressants, anti-psychotics, anti-anxiety medications, and hypnotics. I often ask the audience during seminars on person-centered care, if they would prefer Southern deep-fried chicken and biscuits or Prozac if they're feeling a little down. What do you think they want more? They want the crispy, greasy, deep-fried chicken! Good nutrition can lead to a reduction in falls, which can be costly, and better skin integrity. The bottom line is this: residents can eat well, maintain their health, and enjoy enhanced dining services, and your facility can remain within budget or save money in a number of clinical areas.

Clinical Expenses and Savings

Many facilities that have adopted person-centered care or another model of culture change report improved health and clinical outcomes such as reduced falls, fewer pressure sores, a decrease in the amount of psychotropic medications used, and fewer UTIs—all leading to increased savings. Falls and accidents can lead to further complications for elderly and medically compromised residents, which can lead to higher costs for the facility. Skin care is another cost that can be reduced by better care and nutrition. Many facilities report a decrease in the prescriptions used for depression and behavioral disturbances after moving to a person-centered model, which also reduces costs. When staff is working more closely with residents, they can learn their patterns and daily routines, which can lead to a decrease in incontinence and a reduction in incontinence products.

Better clinical outcomes can lead to increased resident, family, and staff satisfaction, which in time can lead to increased census and income for the facility. Bad care is expensive, and person-centered care is one way to improve outcomes and income. Delivering this kind of care can also reduce liability claims and produce better survey outcomes. Any way you look at it, person-centered care can produce positive outcomes clinically and financially.

Environmental Changes: Costs and Potential Earnings

According to the literature and discussions I have had with numerous administrators, the most expensive aspect of culture change involves physical renovations, retrofitting, or new construction. Despite this, the cost, they say, is well worth it. Redesigning the traditional and institutional facility into a place that is more like home or at least a 5-star hotel is one of the major goals of person-centered care and culture change. The environment that residents are a part of every day has a profound influence on their mood, appetite, energy levels, and overall quality of life. Therefore, altering the environment as much as possible is a critical, albeit expensive step in producing a place where they want to live and where employees want to work.

Redesigning the facility into a home will also give you a competitive advantage over other companies who have not yet engaged in culture change. Grant and McMahon report, "From the beginning, RCCI [Resident-Centered Care Initiative] facilities were more profitable. They had greater revenue, better earnings, higher occupancy rates, and a more favorable payer mix than non-RCCI facilities" (p. 36).

What holds administrators and owners/operators back from investing capital in major building renovations or new construction? They may be afraid of the estimated costs reports they receive from architects and worry about how long it will take to recoup such costs. They may also be concerned when they look at their current revenues and expenses, not taking into account what kind of revenues they could be taking in after construction is finished. They, too, could be shortsighted concerning other expenses that may be reduced after developing a full person-centered program in their facility. What they need to focus on is potential income in the near future, because it will probably be much better than they think. They need to think about having a full house with a waiting list as well as increased quality of living for residents and quality of work for employees. As Arneill and Frasca-Bealieu state: "The design and construction of healthcare facilities is only one of a number of critical components that can change a frightening institution into one that has a supportive and nurturing environment" (p. 163).

Deciding where to start making physical changes is a challenging task, so it is important to remember this—it is not the design *per se* that is the focus, but how the design and environment in general support your residents' quality of life. Take your person-centered committee and a few residents outside of the building and truthfully evaluate what needs a facelift. Start with the exterior of the structure. What does it look like to a passerby? Does it look like a big house, hotel, resort, or an institution? How about the parking lot and landscaping? Every home should have a yard, trees, and gardens. When you walk into the facility, how do the reception area and front lobby present themselves? Are they family and visitor friendly? Do you get the impression that you have just walked into someone's home or a hospital?

Managers may not like this advice, but critically examine how much space is taken up by their offices and other areas and discuss how that space can be converted into resident living space. You may need to physically tear down walls and start from scratch in the front areas of the building. Removing nurses' stations and creating additional resident space will also require architectural redesign and capital investment. Does your facility have any sacred area in it for residents, families, or employees to use for prayer or meditation? Many newer hospitals, especially Planetree Hospitals, and other healthcare centers are building non-denominational sacred spaces such as courtyards or terraces that have gardens, fountains, and benches. Some are simply remodeling a room into a sacred place. Are there plenty of exits to patios, decks, picnic tables, gazebos, outdoor grills, or other outdoor living spaces for residents and staff to use? There may be some capital investments involved with these items as well.

Two of the main areas of the facility that will involve capital investments are the dining room and kitchen. Most long-term care facilities have a large dining room that is designed to seat between 50 to 100 residents. This was the industry standard and considered appropriate and acceptable for many years, but this has changed. The newer theme in designing dining rooms is "smaller is better" for lots of obvious reasons such as lower noise, less stimulation, and a better quality dining experience. This will involve building up to three or four smaller dining areas within the large dining room you already have in the building. There will definitely be costs involved in the redesign but the benefits are well worth it.

The kitchen is another area that may need updated or made more resident and family friendly. This may depend on which styles of person-centered dining you plan on rolling out, such as buffet, family-style, restaurant dining, room service, or other types discussed previously in this book. You may need to purchase steam tables and other mobile equipment, chef and wait staff uniforms, menus, china, silverware and glassware, and linen table clothes and napkins. You may also have to add electrical outlets and plumbing to areas of the facility for buffets, kitchenettes, and snack carts.

Many facilities do not have family or kid friendly areas, but I believe they are greatly needed and would be beneficial for everyone. Think of this area as an additional "family room," just like the one you have in your home. It is a place for family and especially younger children to relax with residents, staff, or by themselves. Expenses involved may include comfortable homelike furniture, a large flat-screen television, gaming systems such as the Nintendo Wii and the Sony Playstation, a computer with Internet access, a library of movies, a bookshelf, and a desk area. The benefits of a family room in your building are endless, but one of the most obvious is that adults can visit their loved one while their children have something to do. There will be no need to find a babysitter because the children don't like nursing homes. Not only is this a good investment and common sense—it changes the very culture of nursing homes into something more friendly and desirable for everyone involved.

One of the final areas where capital investments may be made is the resident's room. Most facilities are providing private rooms and a few semi-private rooms.

I believe residents should have a choice, but if you want to create a place that is more like home, private may be the way to go. I have also seen some facilities redesign standard rooms into "companion suites," which are large enough for two residents (i.e., married couples) and have a living area separate from the bedroom. The living area contains a small kitchenette, table and chairs, and other household furnishings. The whole point of redesigning any room is to make it look and feel like home and to stay away from any hint of institutional design.

Financial Risks

Risks are a natural part of business. However, you can significantly reduce many risks by approaching financial investments wisely and in a well calculated way. Always remember this: no risks, no gain. Don't fall into the trap of believing that you can't upgrade your building or put things off because "the company won't go for it." Design an intelligent plan and present it with confidence. Remind the owners that they cannot afford to ignore your ideas and not make person-centered changes—they will fall behind in the industry.

Some of the financial uncertainties involve spending a good amount of money but then backsliding to the same kind of care your staff provided prior to reconstruction. Building costs are only one aspect of person-centered care and culture change. If fundamental changes in attitude do not take place with redesigning the facility, you may be wasting your money. Let the new construction act as a symbol of a new beginning to you and your staff, and remind them that a person-centered home is more healing and nurturing to residents. It is also a much more pleasant place to work.

Another risk is not completing the entire plan and only going halfway with new designs and ideas. Person-centered design isn't something, in my opinion, that you can half do. It takes a huge commitment financially and emotionally. Choose wisely those areas that you wish to remodel first, watch for the benefits in resident quality of life and employee attitudes, and then move onto the next project as soon as possible.

One of the greatest risks concerning person-centered care in general and financially is lack of leadership and vision. If you do not have the positive driving force of a strong team behind the project, you may be in real trouble. Leadership must be onboard and believe in what they are taking part. They are, after all, redesigning long-term care culture itself. This is no small task, but is indeed an incredibly noble one. Your team is part of something great, and leadership must always remember this and communicate it to members of the team.

Another area that cannot be ignored because the risks are too great is staff development and training. Employees must be educated on person-centered care and culture change as well as how all of the new designs will be used. It would be a massive waste if you spend hundreds of thousands of dollars on beautiful construction but employees carry on as if they were in the same old building. This simply cannot be allowed! Involve employees in every step of the project and explain "why" things are taking place the way they are in the facility. Design training programs on person-centered care, especially in care changes, dining changes, and activities. Don't fall into the trap of believing just because you have a nicer structure your staff will deliver better care. As a matter of fact, you may actually experience more turnover during this process because some employees will not want to deliver person-centered care. Kindly tell them, "See you later!" as you show them the door.

Adding It Up

Money is on everyone's mind, but do not let it stop you from examining the possibilities that person-centered care can create. Some creative financing may be in order, but the only thing that can prevent person-centered care from materializing is you. Person-centered care is an investment in a better way of life for your residents and a better way to work for your staff. It can actually improve the community as a whole. Using money wisely is a challenge and requires looking at financials in a fresh way. Break away from the thought, "We have to make do with what we've got." Strategically examine ways to put person-centered improvement projects together. Examine labor costs, dietary, clinical, and environmental costs now and how money can be saved or earned after person-centered care is implemented. Despite some obvious financial risks, smart owners and operators are investing now because they don't want to become antiquated and left twenty years behind their competition. Do you?

POINTS TO PONDER

1. How does your organization feel about spending money to make significant person-centered and culture change improvements throughout the facility?

2. How would you describe employee turnover in your facility? High? Low? Which department has the highest turnover and why? Does employee turnover impact the quality of care in the facility? Does the facility have a problem with absentee-ism?

3. How much food is thrown away each day? If you answer "a lot", why?

4. Does the facility spend a lot of money on dietary supplements?

5. What percentage of residents receives psychotropic medications?

6. What are some of the greatest risks that may set back progress to your facility becoming a person-centered home?

CHAPTER TEN:
HOW REGULATIONS SUPPORT PERSON-CENTERED CARE AND CULTURE CHANGE

Hell, there are no rules here—we're trying to accomplish something.

Thomas A. Edison

Some healthcare professionals believe that the OBRA regulations do not support person-centered care or culture change. Although the long-term care industry is one of the most regulated in the United States (some say second only to nuclear power) nothing could be further from the truth. In my opinion, many of us may be guilty of over-interpreting or misinterpreting state and federal regulations. I believe that some long-term care professionals simply have never read the regulations and don't know them. There are occasional horror stories circulating throughout the community how surveyors punished facilities that implement new person-centered programs and ultimately got into trouble for it. The only thing that can get in the way of you creating and implementing person-centered care is you. Resting on our laurels and believing that "this is the way we have always done things here" and "why change things now?" can get in the way of providing a much better way of life for residents. Don't use the regulations as an excuse to not implement person-centered care, because they do support it and reflect the core values involved in it.

Despite this, some writers have varying opinions and experiences regarding regulations and culture change. Baker, in her book *Old Age in a New Age: The Promise of Transformative Nursing Homes* finds that the regulations do support culture change. "The federal bureaucracy has also given culture change its blessing. Surveyors are told to accept innovation, rather than penalize it, if residents' quality of life is enhanced. State and long-term care ombudsman, who respond to complaints by residents and families and who advocate on their behalf, now see cultural transformation as a way to overcome decades of abuse and neglect" (p. 203). Dionne Nicole, LNHA, also believes that the regulations support person-centered care and has successfully gone through three annual state surveys since her team implemented their program. She says, "The state survey team was very excited about the changes we were putting in place. Before we would put a particular change in place, we would review the licensure and regulations to assure that we are in compliance. There have been very few times when we were unable to introduce a new change because of the regulations. I believe they actually encourage person-centered care and independence (2008)".

Rantz and Flesner make some good points about regulations and culture change. They remind us, "One of the challenges of experimenting and trying innovations in nursing homes is that compliance with state licensing and federal regulations is still expected of the home" (p. 29). Therefore, it is important that the interdisciplinary team communicate and work closely with surveyors and ombudsmen when thinking about changes in the facility. Don't be afraid to educate the surveyors about what you know and what you want to do for your residents. Create instructional materials for them to take back to their office to share with fellow surveyors and ombudsmen. The more you share, the fewer problems you will face in the future. Make a strong effort to educate your employees regarding all of the changes being made and the regulations that support them. You don't want a surveyor to ask, "Why are residents not awake yet and it's already 9:15 a.m.?" and your employee responds "I don't know!" They should be fully informed and ready to answer intelligently about new approaches and benefits to care.

Other advocates of culture change believe that not only is the nursing home system broken and in need of serious change, the survey and enforcement system is also broken. Shields and Norton stress in their book *In Pursuit of the Sunbeam: A Practical Guide to Transformation from Institution to Household* that compliance does not equal quality of life. "[I]t is not unusual for facilities ... to be deficiency-free and have solid survey compliance and performance. If they comply with the regulations, their slate is clean. No matter that people are awakened on a time schedule, bathed by hoist and dip, and lined up for rigidly scheduled mealtimes" (p. 19).

This is one of the serious flaws about the survey process. Just because a resident goes to physical therapy, eats, showers, and receives medications on time doesn't mean that he or she is happy, has purpose or meaning in life, and is looking forward to waking up tomorrow. It is still very difficult to capture and quantify quality of life in other ways than clinical compliance. Despite this, the authors also believe that person-centered care and culture change are supported by OBRA. They point out another flaw with the survey process—it can be punitive to facilities and this doesn't encourage or produce positive results. "While regulations are necessary, punitive oversight systems are not the answer for improving long-term care. Punitive systems have shown no history of creating positive change in any setting, yet we keep sharpening the teeth of the nursing home regulatory system" (p. 19).

If you believe in person-centered care and culture change, do your homework, communicate with regulators, and do what you think is best for your residents. Shields and Norton also believe that pioneering organizations simply must take regulatory risks and warn us to not become too complacent after we have made significant changes in our facilities. "During an advanced phase of organizational evolution, successful House-hold Model (and other culture change organizations) can be become so relaxed in the comfortable, homey environments that they have created, they become too lax in meeting basic standards of practice" (p. 21). They suggest that regulators and providers come together and work towards an equilibrium, but ultimately survey-ors can neither produce nor prevent culture change. It is up to us to make dramatic and lasting changes in long-term care.

Resident Rights

The regulations support resident rights, which in turn reinforce person-centered care and culture change. Residents living in nursing homes have the right to many choices according to OBRA. Regulation F242 (Self-Determination and Participation) states that residents have the right to schedules, activities, and anything that is important to them. It supports choices of schedules, routines, activities, dining, and participa-tion in the community. As indicated by F246 (Accom-modation of Needs), the nursing home environment should accommodate resident's needs and prefer-ences. It should also be therapeutic, clean, comfort-able, and homelike. F151 (Resident Rights Regulation) clearly indicates that residents have civil rights just like any other citizen, including refusing any kinds of treat-ments (F155). In accordance with F240 (Quality of Life), residents should be assisted by the facility to attain their optimal quality of life and quality of care (F309). A strong OBRA theme, in fact, is that quality of life and freedom of choice are just as important as the quality of care delivered in the facility. Not only do these regulations support person-centered care, they represent some of its most important core values: quality of life and care, decision-making and rights, personal needs and preferences, flexibility, and purpose in life.

Dignity and the Regulations

Among the many themes of OBRA, dignity is one that truly supports person-centered care and culture change, and there are specific regulations that clearly spell this out. F241 (Dignity) is an important regulation and stresses the importance of choices over resident schedules. This can be interpreted to include resident choice concerning natural waking and retiring, when medications are given, when meals are served, shower and bath times, and choice of activities. In other words, residents have the freedom to choose their own schedules.

F246, as discussed above, is concerned with adjusting the environment to meet individual needs. This regulation in particular supports redesigning or rebuilding the physical environment to make it more like home, a 5-star hotel, or something much nicer than a traditional, institutional nursing home. Residents also have the right to participate in their care plans and voice their opinions, desires, and preferences (F280— Resident Participation in Care Planning), which are all associated with dignity issues. They also have the right to individualized activities (F248) which can be interpreted in a number of person-centered ways including spontaneous, 24-hour a day activities, spiritual rights, and almost any activity that brings purpose and meaning to the resident's life.

F241 (Dignity) supports care that enhances full recognition of the resident's individuality, dining changes, and activities. It also supports grooming, dress, activities, independence in dining, private space and property, and social status. This regulation sounds person-centered to me because it makes the person the center of the care process—it is all about his or her psychosocial self as an individual who maintains preferences in dining and activities.

Quality of Life and the Regulations

I believe that the OBRA regulations fully support quality of living in long-term care and are person-centered in both theory and practice. F240 (Quality of Life) promotes quality of life through an environment that humanizes and individualizes each resident. F240, as discussed above, provides support for quality of life for each resident in the facility. Quality of life is also supported through F242 (Self-Determination and Participation) in that each resident has the right to choose activities, schedules, and health care that is consistent with his or her interests; each resident also has the right to interact with people in the community and to make significant decisions about aspects of his or her life in the facility.

If you think about these regulations critically, they do indeed support person-centered care, but I think that there is something much more important than this. Embedded within these regulations is the assumption that employees know the resident and understand what each one wants for his or her own life. To know the resident and appreciate individual needs, preferences, and values is at the heart of person-centered care and culture change.

The Environment and Regulations

Some healthcare professionals worry that all of the physical changes they plan to make will not be supported by the regulations, so they never get their plans off the ground. Once again, the regulations support a comfortable, homelike atmosphere where residents can achieve the highest quality of living. F252 (Homelike Environment) completely supports de-institutionalizing the environment and creating a place that looks and feels like home. The regulation supports residents and families to bring in furniture and other personal items as well as the personalization of each resident room. OBRA and person-centered care are right on track concerning a homelike environment and a less institutional facility. One area that we must be careful about concerns K72 (Life Safety Code) and make sure that no furnishings (from the facility or from families) obstructs any exits. F246 (Accommodation of Needs), as stated above, reinforces an environment that accommodates the needs and preferences of residents.

Some facilities are changing over from traditional resident call light systems to wireless or silent call systems. According to Carmen S. Bowman, these are acceptable according to F463 (Resident Call System) (p. 28). Facilities may choose to use more modern technologies including wireless pagers that are carried by universal employees. Others are using a newer form of handheld radio or cell phone system whereby the resident call is delivered straight to the caregiver's device. One of the greatest benefits from these systems is noise reduction and fewer institutional sounds throughout the building. I am aware of some facilities that have instituted this technology and they have had positive results. Employees are made responsible for their own cell phone or silent pager and so far, no one has lost one. One facility has done away with overhead paging altogether and has replaced it with soft ambient music in the background. It is definitely a pleasant change and makes for a more homelike environment.

Dining Changes and the Regulations

As discussed before, dining is one of the most exciting areas of person-centered care and culture change because there are endless possibilities regarding food choices, presentation, and the dining experience. There are regulations that support resident-centered dining and some regulations that are very important to know so that you don't mistakenly violate them. F368 (Frequency of Meals) supports resident-centered dining and states that three meals are provided per day at regular and normal times. It also states that no more than fourteen hours should pass between the last meal of the day and breakfast the next day. Snacks should always be offered. There is nothing in this regulation that would interfere with any style of dining we have discussed in this book. F242 supports open dining because it is the self-determination regulation stating that residents have the right to make individual choices about dining styles and how long they wish to sleep in before eating breakfast. Remember, the regulations and person-centered care are all about resident choices and their rights to autonomy.

If you choose to implement buffet-style dining, the regulations support it. Just be careful about infection control (F441) and food temperature (F371). If your staff would like to offer restaurant-style dining on a regular basis, there is nothing holding you back. There are, in fact, no regulations that prohibit restaurant-style dining in long-term care. Although you may want to offer this option to cognitively alert residents, I encourage it throughout the entire house and especially on any dementia or behavior unit. In my opinion, everyone has the right to good food and a quality dining experience in long-term care.

There is one style of dining that you do have to be particularly careful about—family-style dining. According to F441 (Infection Control), family-style dining may not be suitable for all residents, especially those who are severely cognitively or mentally impaired. F371 is concerned with the storage, distribution, and serving of foods under sanitary conditions. Food temperature is another issue to consider. Try to use thermal serving bowls when possible. "Keep in mind that neither the regulations nor interpretive guidelines state that food must remain the 140 degrees F on the plate at all times" (Bowman, p. 25). When serving a baked lasagna to your family, does it remain the same temperature at all times while it is sitting in the middle of the table? Does anyone seem bothered when they go back for seconds and it is not the same temperature as it was when it came out of the oven? Of course not! What is important to remember is that foods are served at temperatures that residents find palatable and enjoyable. Hot foods should be hot and cold foods should be cold. One way to support family-style dining is to talk to your residents and ask them if they like it. Document their quotes and present this to surveyors if they question you about family-style dining.

There are also no regulations preventing your facility from providing a liberalized diet to residents. F365 supports it and states that food should be prepared in a form designed to meet individual needs. F242 is concerned with self-determination and also supports the rights residents have to choose what they want to eat, how much they want to eat, and how they want to eat. F370 stresses that food is obtained from sources considered satisfactory by federal, state, or local authorities. I know of some facilities that choose to purchase fresh fruits and vegetables from farm markets during spring and summer months. F370 supports this, and all foods do not have to be ordered from vendors.

Medication Carts and the Regulations

This is a touchy subject for some nurses whom I've told to "throw away your med cart!" When I ask some nurses if there are regulations stating that meds must be passed with med carts their answer is, "Yes, of course there are regulations about that." There are, in fact, no regulations about the use of med carts in long-term care facilities. Sometimes we confuse "traditions" with regulations. The use of med carts is more of a tradition and has become very popular because of efficiency and effectiveness, not because they are mandatory through state or federal regulations. Med carts have become the standard in nursing homes and have been seen by many to be the best way to pass meds.

Many homes that are moving towards person-centered care and culture change are doing away with their med carts and are creating new, more creative ways to pass meds. I speak to many nurses who are in their fifties, sixties, and seventies, and they remember the days when there were no med carts. "We used to put pills in little paper cups on a silver tray and pass them wearing white gloves." What's wrong with doing that again? Some facilities are building lock-boxes in each resident room that contain the resident's medication and chart. Other facilities have designed a nurses' office where residents come to the nurse for their medications. Each of these can be beneficial on particular units or areas of the facility. Be creative and remember to do what is best for the resident—not you.

Make sure that medications are secure and that you meet the "one hour" rule for administration of medications. Instead of assigning a time for each medication as is traditionally done, put the following statements on the Medication Administration Records (MAR): "medications to be given upon natural rising," "medications to be given in the a.m.," "medications to be given at hs," or "medications to be given in the p.m." We are the ones who tell the pharmacy to put specific times on medications, but this is no longer necessary with person-centered care.

Staffing and the Regulations

Questions have been raised by many healthcare professionals concerning cross-trained person-centered specialists or universal employees and using consistent assignments. The good news is that there are no regulations concerning any of these issues. There are no regulations prohibiting consistent staffing, self-assignment, or choice of neighborhoods in which employees wish to work. In fact, these types of practices with employees produce a number of very positive outcomes including greater familiarity with residents, increased comfort between residents and employees, decreased behaviors and need for psychotropic medications, better relationships with family members, improved attendance, fewer call-offs, and decreased turnover.

Cross-training is also being used by many person-centered homes. I particularly like cross-training because it tears down the traditional hierarchy in long-term care, with administration on top, middle managers in the middle, and floor staff on the bottom of the pyramid. I have spoken to a director of nursing who thinks that all administrative and management staff should also be cross-trained to do anything necessary in the facility from direct care, to dining, housekeeping, and activities. Cross-trained employees take care of their own neighborhood and eight to ten residents living in that neighborhood. It is good for customer service, quality of care, and overall quality of life.

Adding It Up

It should be clear that the regulations support person-centered care and culture change and that only you and your team can hold yourselves back from making significant and lasting changes in your facility. I highly advise that you get your local and state regulators and surveyors on board immediately on your journey to person-centered care. Educate them on the changes that you wish to make and do your homework on new trends and changes that are taking place across the country. Invite the ombudsman and volunteer ombudsman to assist you along the way. They would be a great resource in helping your staff with all of the resident interviews, surveys, and data gathering necessary to make resident-centered changes. And last, with all change comes risk. That's life. You can minimize much of the risk factor by researching and learning as much as possible and getting others involved. Do not let the risks frighten you away from creating a culture of compassion and dignity for your residents. They deserve it.

POINTS TO PONDER

1. Does your management staff generally believe that the regulations support or get in the way of person-centered care?

2. Is fear of the regulations holding your facility back from starting culture change?

3. After reading this chapter, do you feel better about the regulations and how they support person-centered care?

CHAPTER ELEVEN:
THE NECESSITY OF LEADERSHIP IN CULTURE CHANGE

If your actions inspire others to dream more, learn more, do more and become more, you are a leader.

John Quincy Adams

One of the final and most important components of person-centered care and culture change is strong, effective leadership. There are a wide variety of ways that leadership can be discussed, but for the purpose of this book, I choose to present it differently, focusing almost exclusively on the kind of leadership necessary to change the culture of your facility and get everyone onboard with you. Leadership can make or break how effectively you and your staff design and implement person-centered care, so I cannot stress enough how critical leadership is in culture change. Specifically, strong leadership will involve commitment to change, getting out of your comfort zone, empowering your employees, leaving old management styles behind, and embracing a new style of leadership (which I call the "Steering Agent") becoming a servant leader, and using the law of attraction.

Making the Commitment to Change: Person-Centered Leadership

Change must begin with the leadership of your facility. Person-centered care involves a change in attitudes and philosophies about resident care and quality of life. It is therefore necessary for leadership to believe in the values of person-centered care and to become a role model of such values. Employees, as a rule of thumb, do not want to work any harder than their management, and will not believe in something that their leaders do not. Effective person-centered leadership involves believing that residents are important people who deserve to live a fulfilling life and should experience growth every day of their lives, regardless of their physical or cognitive disorders. It requires a belief that compassion and care are just as important as treatment. Leadership also involves helping employees change their ideas about the facility itself—namely that the building is the resident's home and they are paid guests. The facility does not "belong" to employees. Instead, it belongs to the residents. Leaders must drive the idea of "home" throughout each phase of culture change and encourage their staff to abandon old, institutional ways of viewing residents and the facility.

To achieve this, leaders must encourage their staff to get to know the residents they are caring for and to form genuine relationships with them. During the process of change, leaders must be confident and equipped to deal effectively with resistance from managers, employees, families, residents and other healthcare professionals in the community. Great leaders must keep an open mind concerning all of the changes we have addressed in this book, including dining changes, activities, how care is delivered, physical changes to the building, how dementia care is delivered, how staff perceive families (they are not visitors!), dealing with the budget, and regulations. I know this is a lot to handle, but perhaps there has never been a better time for you to step up your game and become a better leader.

Rantz and Flesner believe that leadership should be dedicated and committed to deinstitutionalizing the organization, to the basic values of person-centered care, to flexibility in how person-centered care is designed in your facility, and to respect for residents and employees (pp. 39-49). They point out that commitment to residents involves a respect for their established lifelong patterns, for their connections to the wider community, for their opportunities to achieve personal goals, for honoring individual requests, for close and personal relationships with employees, for high levels of family satisfaction, for choice in living environment, social events, and personal celebrations, and for continued contributions to society. Commitment to employees involves maintaining open communication, decentralized decision-making, autonomy for staff at all levels, opportunities for STNAs to advance their careers, support for employees and their personal lives, recognition and reward for great work, encouragement to develop genuine relationships with residents, consistent assignment, and empowerment of all staff. One way to achieve all of these commitments and many more is to get out of your comfort zone as a leader or manager and expand your own horizons.

Leaving Your Comfort Zone

Sometimes to be your best, you must stop and evaluate yourself as a leader or a manager and ask critical questions about your style of leadership and its effectiveness. Have you become somewhat complacent in your career or in the facility? Are things running so smoothly that you don't see any need for change? I tell many audiences at my seminars that all leaders need continual growth because we are much like a piece of fruit growing on a tree. As long as we take in rain and sunshine, we continue to grow. But once we stop taking in what we need, we fail to grow, begin to rot, and eventually fall off the tree. Rotten fruit is good to no one.

So, exactly how do you leave your comfort zone and start to improve as a leader? A good way to start is to stop feeling comfortable in your position and begin to embrace change. Don't resist change. Instead, take chances and get your staff excited about the possibilities that person-centered care can have for everyone in the facility and the community. The next step in leaving your comfort zone is to educate yourself not only on person-centered care and culture change ideas, but on new leadership styles that you have never known about or have been too busy to consider trying. There is a lot of great information out there on change leadership, talent management, motivation management, the self-motivated workforce, and others. Challenging yourself with a new style of leadership can help you out of your comfort zone because you will need to learn new skills sets that you may have never used before.

Another important step in leaving your comfort zone is to embrace the unknown and get ready for new and exciting things to happen not only to yourself, but to your team and residents. Many people are afraid of change because they are unsure of what it can lead to or what is on the other side of change. Don't let fear hold you back from becoming bigger and better than you are now. There are risks involved in leaving your comfort zone, but without risks there is no growth. Other people may not leave their comfort zone because they believe that they can't and this is a sad fact. There are people who do not believe in themselves, and therefore, no one else does. They don't try to improve because they feel they can't. You must not only embrace the unknown but believe that you can change and become a better leader. If you believe in yourself, others will also. In other words, change requires confidence.

The final step in leaving your comfort zone is to sit back and watch what happens. Keep a critical eye on how employees react to you. Do they seek you out more often? Do they want to be around you rather than run away from you? People find what they are looking for in life, so keep an open mind to the changes that are evolving around you after you have left your comfort zone and have starting using new ideas and approaches to leadership. Only you can make yourself the person you want to become.

Empowering Employees

When I discuss empowering employees at seminars and training sessions, I ask the audience to define empowerment. Some respond, "Giving employees control," or "Not micromanaging employees." While these are good ways to describe empowerment, I follow up by saying that we have thrown this term around so much that it has become watered down to the point where most people either don't know what it means or don't believe that they can become empowered to be their own person at work. True empowerment involves educating your staff on person-centered care, trusting that they will use their experience and wisdom to do the right things, and then letting go. The ultimate goal of employee empowerment is a self-managed and self-scheduling workforce that requires little to no supervision.

What will you need to empower your employees with concerning person-centered care and culture change? All empowerment requires education and training, so the best place to start is teaching your staff about each component of person-centered care. Once they have a general idea, it's time to let them use their creativity and spontaneity in delivering the best care they can in ways they have always wanted.

Empower your staff with the core values and principles discussed in this book. Encourage them to create a culture of care with their attitudes and philosophies. Empower your employees to create a home for their residents and discourage institutionalized care. Encourage them to sit down and eat with the residents they care for in their neighborhoods. Encourage them to engage in play and celebration. Promote the idea of spontaneous activities twenty-four hours a day. Persuade them to be flexible and to let life flow naturally in the facility. Empower your nursing assistants to become "person-centered specialists," and give them a boost to their ego and self-esteem.

Encourage all staff to find places in the facility that look too institutional and ask residents how they would like to redesign these areas. Motivate staff to challenge themselves and rethink how care should be delivered to residents diagnosed with dementia and Alzheimer's disease. Promote the philosophy to your staff that families are not visitors, but family members and partners coming to visit their loved ones in their home. Challenge your staff to become more involved with families and to get to know and understand them as much as possible.

Empower your management team to look at and improve labor costs, dietary expenses, clinical expenses, and costs involved in environmental changes throughout the facility. Promote the idea that there is no growth without risk and that their calculated risks will be supported by administration. Give your employees the confidence they need to provide person-centered care the way they believe is right, especially during annual state surveys. Encourage them to teach surveyors about their own brand of person-centered care and to explain why they choose to do it this way. These, I believe, are the best ways to empower employees at every level concerning person-centered care and culture change.

Empowering means permitting employees to make their own decisions. Those who work closest to the resident, the STNAs, universal employees, or person-centered specialists, need to be empowered because they will know more about residents than anyone else in the facility. It only makes sense that they speed up the decision-making process without seeking management or supervisors to make decisions for them. Empowering them will increase their self-esteem, improve employee satisfaction, and give control to those who deserve it—our employees who work most closely with residents. Empowering them can eliminate frustration and motivate them to own their work even more.

Becoming a "Steering Agent"

Culture change requires not only changing how care is delivered and physical modifications to the building but a philosophical change in how management perceives their role in that new culture. I have lectured hundreds of times on the challenge to remove our traditional notions of what management means and the roles managers play in health care. The challenge is to let go of control and forget trying to "manage" employees. I have met many managers who cannot manage themselves, let alone a department or dozens of employees. This has led me to a term that I prefer using over the term manager—"steering agent." Since we begin our journey with a steering team, why not develop the team into individual steering agents?

In my opinion, a steering agent is an individual in a management or supervisory position who helps guide or steer employees into the right direction concerning care, ethics, quality of life, policies, and regulations. It also involves providing coaching when needed, retraining, and educational support. There are no egos involved in being a steering agent, because the goals are to enhance the employees' capabilities and to maximize their skills and talents as well as improve the living conditions of the residents. No one is actually managing anyone or anything, and employees can be steered into self-management, self-assignment, and eventually self-scheduling. To be a steering agent, one must develop strong relationships, genuine and open communication, and trust with those they steer. An unfortunate fact is that some managers today do not truly know their employees, aren't confident in their skills or abilities, do not communicate well with them, and ultimately do not trust them. Being a steering agent is relationship intensive, just like person-centered care.

Training managers, supervisors, and administrative staff to become steering agents is a key ingredient in developing a successful and lasting culture of care. Training begins with the transformation from management to leadership, because steering agents are true leaders, not managers. Leaders are more concerned with results, not the busywork that is involved in achieving results. They keep their eye on the big picture—culture change and a person-centered home. They allow employees to utilize their skill, experience, education, and brain cells to deliver care and quality of living to those for whom they care—their residents. They are able to manage themselves and act as motivators in a charismatic and engaging way.

A steering agent always observes and critically thinks about how work can be improved for employees, how employees can work smarter, not harder, and how employees can maximize their time throughout the day so that they can spend quality time with residents. No longer is "looking busy" a key element of daily work life—instead relaxing, playing, celebrating, and enjoying life with the residents are the main job descriptors of person-centered specialists. Leaders seek the truth, so they have constant dialogue with employees concerning areas that can be improved. They seek opinions and ideas from those working the front lines in the home. They also give authority and power to others who are engaged most closely with residents. They allow employees to call the shots and make mistakes. They provide support at all times regardless of outcomes.

Steering agents also use mistakes as teaching moments and act as educators by providing information that can help employees better themselves. Steering agents are researchers who constantly review current literature in areas of long-term care, Alzheimer's disease and dementia, aging, nursing, social work, therapy, nutrition, and other topics. They seek to develop a more intelligent and prepared work force. They also train their replacement and do not allow egos to get in the way of cultural improvement. Real leaders want to move on to bigger and better things in their professional lives and freely transmit their knowledge and experience to others who may one day hold their position. In this way, leaders are generous with their knowledge, skill, and experience.

Steering agents and great leaders want their employees to be self-led, self-managed, and eventually self-sufficient. This represents an organizational belief in a flat and even playing field—a flat organizational map. There is no traditional top-down management, pyramid of hierarchical power, or hands-off leadership. Instead, employees have a voice, make meaningful choices, and are assisted by people who are willing to steer and train them and eventually replace managers. Instead of trying to manage or control a group of employees, they are driven by purpose and meaning. When barriers to quality do arise, they find ways to eliminate them and move forward.

Servanthood Leadership

Another excellent form of leadership that can be taught to managers, supervisors, and administrative staff is servanthood leadership. Although there are numerous styles and forms of leadership, I believe this one fits in well with the values and principles of person-centered care and culture change. John C. Maxwell and James A. Aurtey among many other authors and business leaders have written about and taught servanthood leadership. Maxwell believes, "You've got to love your people more than your position," because being a leader really has nothing to do with the position. It is about serving the people you manage, supervise, or lead. It is an attitude that leadership is about serving others and not one's self. This completely supports the kind of leadership that is needed in long-term care in general, but particularly in facilities that adopt person-centered care. According to Maxwell, the qualities of a servanthood leader include willingness to put others ahead of one's own agenda, confidence, initiating service to others, caring little about one's title or position, and serving out of love. He states, "If you want to lead on the highest level, be willing to serve on the lowest" (p. 133).

In his book *The Servant Leaders: How to Build and Create Team, Develop Great Morale, and Improve Bottom-Line Performance*, Autry outlines what he believes are the essential characteristics of the servanthood leader (pp. 3-20). First and foremost, leadership is more about caring for people, not controlling them. It is more about being present and available, not just being the boss. It has nothing to do with territoriality, but instead involves a willingness to let go of one's ego, tap into one's spirit, and being one's most authentic self. It is not about pep talks or empty rhetoric. It is instead about creating a happy and meaningful work culture. Servanthood leaders pay attention to people, and they lead with love. All of these characteristics completely support the kind of leadership that is needed in person-centered care facilities.

Using the Law of Attraction as a Leadership Style

The final type of leadership that I want to address in this chapter relates to something that I have talked about at many seminars and workshops, lectures, and conversations with friends and colleagues. It is based on the principle and universal law known as the law of attraction. The essential feature of this law is that people possess energy and a presence by the way they think, act, and behave towards the world. This energy seeks out like energy and draws it back to that person. In other words, like attracts like.

This can be a powerful tool for leaders to use in their daily lives, not only at work, but at home and in their personal lives. I often (unfortunately, too often) hear managers and supervisors complaining about their work and employees. They complain that work is stressful and unfulfilling, filled with trauma and disappointments, and at the end of the day, all they have to show for it is a headache and sore feet. I feel sorry for these people, because they haven't learned *why* all of these things are happening to them. I also hear of managers who grumble about babysitting their employees and dealing with drama, negativity, and multiple complaints in the workplace. None of this can be good for a person-centered environment.

So, how can these leaders turn themselves around and change their perceptions of the world? It is possible through the law of attraction. The truth of the matter is this—these people are negative to begin with, and they are sending out negativity to the workplace. In turn, they are getting exactly what they send out—more negativity, drama, and things to complain about. Have you ever noticed that when you find one negative employee, five more are not far behind? Negativity attracts negativity, and positive attitudes attract healthy, energized and positive attitudes. The energy that we send out to the world is returned to us and is significant in shaping who we are and who we can become.

The law of attraction can significantly improve how leaders operate in long-term care or anywhere else for that matter. Leaders must be positive, healthy-minded individuals who wish to serve others and are not in their leadership position for power or control. They are people who will lead with a can-do attitude, from their hearts and spirits, and will put other employees, families, and residents before themselves. They will use their creativity and imagination to lead and serve others. They will place great emphasis on genuine communication and relationships instead of deadlines, reports, and schedules. By doing this, they will attract the same kinds of attitudes. Positive, healthy attitudes and energy are infectious and will spread to other managers and employees. The law of attraction truly is a person-centered method of providing person-centered care, employee-centered support, and family-centered service.

Adding It Up

The only way to revolutionize quality of care and life in long-term care and develop person-centered services is through not fair or mediocre leadership, but by great and inspiring leadership. This involves making a personal commitment to making change possible in your facility. It also involves truly believing that person-centered care is superior to traditional and institutional care. Becoming a great leader involves stress and challenge—both requiring that you leave your comfort zone and explore new ways of thinking, feeling, and behaving like a leader. You also have to be a leader whom people want to follow, or there is no point to leadership. Inspire your staff to get on board and become significant participants in the process. Empower them to try new things, make mistakes, offer ideas, and take the lead. Steer your staff through complicated issues and dilemmas. Let them succeed the ways they know how, but include your gentle guidance. Serve others and watch the results. Put out positive energy, and get ready to experience the law of attraction.

POINTS TO PONDER

1. How would you characterize the leadership among your administrative staff? Department heads? Supervisors?

2. When is the last time you challenged yourself to leave your comfort zone and learned new ways to lead others?

3. Does your management team empower the employees in your facility? Do the employees feel that they are empowered and supported by the management or do they feel micromanaged?

4. What kinds of energy do you attract to yourself at work? Positive? Negative? What about your co-workers? What kinds of energy do they attract?

CHAPTER TWELVE: THE BENEFITS OF PERSON-CENTERED CARE AND CULTURE CHANGE

*Do the right thing. It will gratify some
people and astonish the rest.*

Mark Twain

Person-centered care can lead to some of the most
desired outcomes for residents, employees, families,
organizations, and entire communities. Unfortunately,
there are not many studies that have evaluated the effectiveness of person-centered care in nursing homes.
Despite this, it can be argued both theoretically and
practically that person-centered care and the development of a compassionate culture of care can bring
about many positive physical, psychological, social,
and spiritual outcomes. The purpose of this chapter is
to give the reader a good overall review of possible
benefits of person-centered care.

Benefits to Residents

A handful of studies have shown desired outcomes of person-centered care including the work of Rantz and Flesner (2004). Their research indicates that the use of disposable briefs, antipsychotic medications, and nutritional supplements all decreased significantly after a long-term care facility implemented person-centered care (p. 37). Disruptive behaviors diminished, unintended weight loss decreased, and low functioning residents became more involved in activities while receiving personalized care from the staff. Food costs declined during the first year of implementation of person-centered care.

When residents feel that they are surrounded by a culture of love and care and have more control over their lives, they may become recipients of a significant amount of positive health outcomes, including increased appetite and improved dining experiences, a decreased need for catheters and adult briefs, a decrease in pressure ulcers and skin wounds, decreased dehydration, a reduction in sleeping medication, and a decrease or elimination of physical restraints. They may become more motivated to participate in their own activities of daily living, engage more in personalized care, and receive improved hospice care. They may receive improved pain management and comply with interventions and treatment plans.

Psychologically, residents who feel more autonomy and independence may experience a decreased need for psychotropic medications. I sometimes ask my audiences at seminars that if they had a choice over Paxil or New York style cheesecake, which would they prefer? Almost all the time, they go for the cheesecake. When residents eat well and have good life satisfaction, there may be no need for many psychotropic drugs. Some residents may actually experience an improved mood and become less depressed and anxious once the environment becomes less institutional and more homelike. They may be less withdrawn and isolated. Boredom and loneliness may become problems of the past. They may sense an overall increase in emotional well-being and personal growth. Stress can be better managed or minimized, and loss can be overcome by a fulfilling life full of choices and challenges.

Another area that may reap great benefit to residents is social life—something that is, in my opinion, sorely lacking in many long-term care facilities. Once the facility is transformed from a hospital-like, institutionalized medical center into a comfortable and welcoming home, residents may begin to enjoy all sorts of social benefits, including control over their own care schedules and personal routines and improved relationships with caregivers, residents, and people in the community. They may become more involved in the life of the home, find greater meaning in life, and experience a new level of life satisfaction. They may find new purposes to live and thrive. I often ask healthcare professionals this question: "If you were a nursing home resident right now, what would make you excited about waking up tomorrow? Is there anything to look forward to? What would you need to maintain purpose in your life in a nursing home?" These are questions we should all ask ourselves and our residents. What gives them purpose and motivation to get out of bed each morning? You may be surprised at the answers you receive.

Eliminating clinical areas such as large and bulky nurses' stations and replacing them with social spaces can give your residents many things to look forward to, depending on what you and your staff do with that space. When in doubt—ask the residents. Instead of nurses' stations, how about coffee shops, book stores, additional lounges, gift shops, soda shops, 1950s-style diners, or something that would be meaningful for the residents? As food quality increases, quality of life will surely increase as well. Give the residents power to choose what to order from vendors and ask them if they would prefer restaurant-style dining, family-style dining, or buffets. All of these features of person-centered care can increase resident's overall sense of social well-being.

Other possible social outcomes to person-centered care include better and more meaningful activities, recreation and events, participating in "spa time" instead of taking a bath or shower, enjoying real privacy either alone or with family or friends, and the ability to have and take care of their beloved pets. Residents can benefit greatly from the ability to engage in more meaningful and significant relationships in an environment that is conducive to social encounters. They can also enjoy practicing and celebrating their own faith with others or in private. In other words, they can live their lives as they wish, just like they would in their own homes.

Benefits to Employees

Residents are not the only ones who will enjoy the many positive outcomes of person-centered care and culture change. Those individuals who have dedicated their careers to the care of frail, elderly, and medically compromised people can also benefit. Employees can benefit by working in a homelike environment that is free of micromanagement and excessive rigidity. They may engage in real teamwork with a group of professionals who share a common vision and are free to act autonomously. Employees will benefit immediately from the new resident-to-staff ratio that most facilities endorse when implementing person-centered care—seven or eight residents per employee. This makes for a much better workload for the person-centered specialist. It also provides numerous opportunities for getting to know residents, forming more genuine relationships, and developing a secondary family. When people work in such close proximity, they may also improve communication, experience personal growth, and enjoy greater autonomy, independence, and creativity. Job satisfaction and greater meaning in one's work can also be welcomed effects of positive culture change.

If employees have the opportunity to practice self-assignment, maintain a permanent schedule, and engage in self-scheduling, they may actually begin to feel like they "own" their jobs and roles in the facility. These are more ways to truly empower employees, as I discussed earlier in this book. If they can take part in designing their own neighborhoods, they may enjoy their work conditions even more. When managers become steering agents, employees may benefit from feeling that they have more support and are more encouraged to try new things and less worried about failure or punishment. Ultimately, person-centered care can become a great source for stress management among employees.

Other benefits of person-centered care include a probable decrease in employee turnover and an increase in employee commitment and dedication. Retaining good employees can save a lot of money that can be used for other things. Employees can also benefit from eating breakfast, lunch, and dinner with their residents and families. People who break bread together have the opportunity for more social interaction and relationship building. Many nursing home employees have told me that they wish their facility had takeout, so that they could bring dinner home to their families after work. When is the last time you heard that? Staff may enjoy fewer battles on shower day because the shower room has been transformed into a beautiful and welcoming spa. I have spoken to many caregivers who would like to use the spa rooms that are in some person-centered care facilities.

We all know that one day roughly 65% of us will require care in a skilled facility either short- or long-term. The baby-boom generation is very aware of this. Many are thankful that person-centered care is making such a positive difference in their facilities, because one day they will be in the bed receiving care from someone they do not know. Baby boomers want better care in buildings that look like houses, 5-star hotels, or resorts—not institutions. Person-centered care also provides the opportunity for death with dignity, having final wishes granted, and receiving tender loving care until death. Hospice services may benefit more from person-centered care. And finally, culture change invites fun, excitement, and enjoyment back into the workplace. It encourages life to be fulfilling to residents and employees. It is okay to have fun at work, laugh with your residents, act goofy, and have play time with them. Person-centered care calls for all of us to lighten up, love, live, and laugh.

Benefits to Families

Families usually go through a fairly rough time when it comes time to place Mom or Dad in a nursing home. No one wants to see that day coming and few are prepared for the emotional impact that day can bring. Therefore, it is essential for you to understand how person-centered care can benefit family members as well as residents and employees. Many homes are designing family and child friendly areas where individuals can rest, socialize, drop off the kids, and visit with their loved one in the comfort of a homey environment. When the building is inviting to families, they are much more likely to visit and engage in the care and lives of their loved ones.

All of the person-centered amenities described in this book can help to diminish feelings of guilt associated with nursing home placement of an elderly family member. The family can experience great customer service and satisfaction in a person-centered environment. They can also be encouraged to form more relationships with other residents, families, and staff. Stress may be decreased within a person-centered home. It helps if your employees reach out to families and adopt the attitude that they are not visitors, but instead are "our" partners—our families. Finally, families can receive benefits in knowing that their loved one lives in a great place, surrounded by loving employees who genuinely care for them. When death finally comes, person-centered care can take some of the sting out of it.

Benefits to the Organization

Homes that have adopted some version of culture change, including person-centered care, have seen many positive outcomes. First and foremost, they are doing the right thing and are providing the best quality of care and life to residents. Because of this, they enjoy fewer complaints from residents, families, employees, and outside agencies. Their reputation is enhanced in the community as an innovative and caring place. They can flatten their organizational structure, which enhances teamwork, promotes better care, improves attitudes and ultimately encourages the development of relationships throughout the building and organization. Person-centered homes may rely less on temporary employees and agencies, reduce liabilities and minimize litigations. They can enhance relationships between the organization and local professionals working for the Area Agency on Aging, ombudsman program, and the Department of Health as well as countless other entities in the community. And finally, as seen in Chapter 9, while person-centered care was never meant to be a cost-saving model or a way to reduce expenses, it does just that—it saves the facility money in countless areas and reduces expenses in areas of waste.

Benefits to the Community

Whether the financial climate is rough or not, a person-centered home can create a viable source of jobs that stimulates the local economy. In some smaller communities, a person-centered home can become the business epicenter and create hundreds of jobs for local citizens. The benefits don't stop there. These homes also feed many smaller companies, vendors, and local businesses, which in turn stimulate the local economy. Besides the obvious financial benefits, person-centered homes can be a great source of pride for the community. Employees can become active in local chambers of commerce, church organizations, and schools. The kinds of support and the relationships that that can be formed are endless and priceless.

Adding It Up

I have attempted to outline some of the most common benefits of person-centered care to residents, employees, the organization and community as a whole. I am sure there are many that are not included in this chapter. The point is that there will be so many benefits to everyone after person-centered care is implemented that an entire book could be written about them. Person-centered care truly is one of the most common-sense, win-win philosophies of care that I have ever seen in my career. Residents can live a more fulfilling and normal life. Employees can take time to be with those they care for and experience a greater level of work satisfaction. Family members may be happier than ever before. Census can benefit by the development of a full house with a waiting list, and the community can be proud of such an exemplary employer in town.

POINTS TO PONDER

1. After reading this chapter, are you more confident that person-centered care can create numerous positive benefits and outcomes for your residents, their families, your employees and the community as a whole?

2. What kinds of benefits do you think your facility would experience soon after implementing person-centered care?

CHAPTER THIRTEEN:
CONCLUDING REMARKS

---

*With malice toward none, with charity for all, with firm-
ness in the right as God gives us to see the right, let
us finish the work we are in.*

Abraham Lincoln

Well, there you have it! I set out to write a comprehensive book on person-centered care and culture change
in nursing homes, and I have come to the end. As I
started this book three years ago, I was disappointed
that there was only a small amount of literature on
these topics, so I set out to learn as much as I could
from healthcare professionals in the field, residents
living in nursing homes, and their family members. I
gathered as much information as I could and began
teaching facilities how to transform their buildings from
traditional medical-based care facilities to person-
centered homes. Within the last three years, more information has come out and some very good books
have been written. I discuss most of them in this book.
Despite that, I was still unsatisfied that there was no

single book or guide that laid out all (or at least most) of the essential components of person-centered care. Even if this resource existed, would it tell us what to implement as well as how to go through the process of transformation? Since there was no book out there, I was motivated to write one.

My goals in writing this book are simple—put as much information as I can about person-centered care in one book, make it readable and enjoyable (I hope!), and write it for everyone who wants to learn and then put these ideas into action. Whether you are an owner/operator, physician, administrator, nurse, social worker, occupational, physical or speech therapist, registered dietician, dietetic manager, nursing assistant, activity professional, housekeeper, or maintenance professional, I hope this book has spoken to you. I also hope that residents, families, clergy, politicians, and anyone who can help change the culture of long-term care has now finished this book and is in some way inspired to do great things with the ideas within it.

There is a lot of information to digest, but each chapter represents an essential element of person-centered care that can be taught to your staff. "Start low and go slow," as some say in psychiatry concerning beginning prescription medications. You may wish to begin by sharing the information in this book with your management, and from there, educate your entire staff through a series of in-services. If there are local workshops or seminars on person-centered topics, try to attend them and get as much information as you can from a variety of sources. After educating yourself and your employees, decide where you want to start making changes.

As I discussed earlier, many homes decide to start in dietary services because everyone notices good food. Your activity director can start training nursing assistants to engage in spontaneous, 24-hour per day activities. Your housekeeping director can train them in deep cleaning and handling and storing chemicals. Nursing can review areas that need to become person-centered, including med pass, care schedules, self-assignment, and creating neighborhoods.

Take a walk around your building now that you have read this book. What do you see through your new set of person-centered eyes? Are there areas that resemble hospitals? Is the place in need of a person-centered face-life? Would you now like to tear out those nurses' stations and make the place more resident and family friendly? Are you thinking now about how to design and deliver person-centered dementia care? How do you feel about families, expenses, regulations, and leadership?

It is my hope that if you don't feel different, you've already begun the process or you are way ahead of the curve, and that would be a good thing. If you do feel different, congratulations! You have been inspired to become an agent of culture change and are beginning to think differently about long-term care. Hopefully you are beginning your journey away from traditional and institutionalized nursing home care and are on your way to a person-centered culture of compassion. This is a great thing! So, what are you waiting for? Take this information and share it with everyone who can benefit from it and please put these ideas into action. Our employees, residents, families, communities—and you—deserve it.

BIBLIOGRAPHY

1) ADA Reports. (2005) "Position of the American Dietetic Association: Liberalization of the Diet Prescription Improves Quality of Life for Older Adults in Long-Term Care." *Journal of the American Dietetic Association*, 105(12).

2) Arneill, Bruce and K. Frasca-Beaulieu. (2003). Healing Environments: Architecture and Design Conducive to Health. In Frampton, Susan, B., Laura Gilpin and Patrick A. Charmel (Eds), Putting Patients First: Designing and Practicing Patient-Centered Care (pp. 163-190). San Francisco: Jossey-Bass.

3) Autry, James, A. (2001). *The Servant Leaders: How to Build and Create Team, Develop Great Morale, and Improve Bottom-Line Performance*. New York: Three Rivers Press.

4) Baker, Beth. (2007). *Old Age in a New Age: The Promise of Transformative Nursing Homes*. Nashville: Vanderbilt University Press.

5) Bowman, Carmen, S. (2006). *Regulatory Support for Culture Change: How OBRA '87 Regulations Support Culture Change*. WI: Action Pact.

6) Brooker, Dawn. 2007. *Person-Centered Dementia Care: Making Services Better*. London: Jessica Kingsley Publishers.

7) Chapin, M. (2006). "Creating Innovative Places: Organizational and Architectural Case Studies of the Culture Change Movement in Long-Term Care." Southern Gerontological Society Annual Meeting, Lexington, KY.

8) Edgman-Levitan, S. and P D Cleary. (1996). What information do consumers want and need? *Health Affairs*, Winter 1996; 15(4): 42-56.

9) Frampton, S.B., Gilpin, L, and Charmel, P.A. (Eds.). (2003). *Putting Patients First: Designing and Practicing Patient-Centered Care*. San Francisco: Jossey-Bass.

10) Goffman, Erving. (1961). *Asylums: Essays on the Social Situation of Mental Patients and other Inmates*. NY: Anchor Books.

11) Grant, L. A. and Edward McMahon. (2008). "Culture Change or Perish: The Business Case." *Provider*, February Issue.

12) Kahana, Eva. (1971). "Emerging Issues in Institutional Services for the Aging." *The Gerontologist*, Spring, Part 1, 51–58.

13) Kane, R.A., Kane, R.L. and R.C. Ladd. (1998). *The Heart of Long-Term Care*. NY: Oxford University Press.

14) Kane, R.A., Lum, T.Y., Cutler, L.J., Degenholtz, H.B., and Tzy-Chyi Yu. (2007). "Resident Outcomes in Small-House Nursing Homes: A Longi-

tudinal Evaluation of the Initial Green House Program." *Journal of the American Geriatrics Society*, 55(6), 832–839.

15) Kitwood, Tom. (1997). *Dementia Reconsidered: The Person Comes First*. Buckingham: Open University Press.

16) Lidtz, C.W., Fischer, L. and R.M. Arnold. (1992). *The Erosion of Autonomy in Long-Term Care*. NY: Oxford University Press.

17) Locher, Julie, Yoels, William, Mauer, Donna, and Jillian Ellis. (2005). "Comfort Foods: An Exploratory Journey into the Social and Emotional Significance of Food." *Food and Pathways*, 13(4), 273–297.

18) Maxwell, John. C. (1999). *The 21 Indispensible Qualities of a Leader: Becoming the Person Others Will Want to Follow*. Nashville: Nelson Business.

19) Mitty, Ethel, L. (2005). "Culture Change in Nursing Homes: An Ethical Perspective." *Annals of Long-Term Care*, 13:3, 47–51

20) Rantz, Marilyn, J., and Marcia K. Flesner (2004). *Person-Centered Care: A Model for Nursing Homes*. Washington DC: nursingbooks.com.

21) Savishinsky, Joel, S. (1991). *The Ends of Time: Life and Work in a Nursing Home*. NY: Bergin and Garvey.

22) Shields, Steve, and La Vrene Norton. (2006). *In Pursuit of the Sunbeam: A Practical Guide to*

Transformation from Institution to Household. NY: Action Pact Press.

23) Tellis-Nayak, V. (2007). "Culture Change: Its Lapses, Anomalies—and Achievements." *Nursing Home Magazine*, May, 22–23.

24) Tellis-Nayak, V. (2007). "A Person-Centered Workplace: The Foundation for Person-Centered Caregiving in Long-Term Care." *Journal of the American Medical Directors Association* (January), 46–54.

25) Thomas, William, H. (1996). *Life Worth Living: How Someone You Love can Still Enjoy Life in a Nursing Home (The Eden Alternative in Action)*. MA: Vander Whk & Burnham.